WHAT WOULD TED LASSO DO?

How Ted's Positive Approach Can Help You

BY
LUCY BROADBENT

Disclaimer

CONTENTS

Introduction 1

1: Believe 7

2: Be Successful .15

3: Be Curious 21

4: Be Optimistic .30

5: Be a Do-Gooder 39

6: Be Open to Therapy 47

7: Be A Good Parent (To Yourself) 56

8: Be More Like a Woman 62

9: Be Forgiving 71

10: Be You 79

11: Be A Good Leader 85

12: Be Kind 92

References 98

INTRODUCTION

BE A GOLDFISH.

A what?

A goldfish.

Why?

Coach Ted Lasso is standing on the side of a soccer field, a whistle around his neck, mud on his shoes. Yes, we did hear him right. He is telling Sam Obisanya to be a goldfish because Sam has just been insulted by Jamie Tartt, one of the other players. It makes no sense. We are as confused as Sam. But then Ted explains that a goldfish is the happiest animal in the world because it has a ten second memory.

That's when we realize that Ted isn't just talking to Sam. He is talking to all of us. Like a cleverly disguised self-help guru, Ted is giving us one of his heartwarming life-lessons. He is telling us to forget about grudges when sharp barbs come our way because it's healthier to shake off an insult than hang onto it.

For those who might have missed Apple TV+'s

award-winning show, Ted Lasso is the lovable American coach, played by Jason Sudeikis, who arrives in the United Kingdom to turn around the fortunes of a fictional Premier League soccer team. You don't need to understand or even like soccer to enjoy the show. Ted doesn't understand the rules either. "Heck, you could fill two internets with what I don't know about football," he tells everyone on arrival at AFC Richmond.

But there's more to *Ted Lasso* than just fish-out-of-water comedy. Hidden deep in the show's DNA are self-improvement lessons which psychologists and life coaches have been studying for decades. The goldfish theory is actually so old that the Chinese philosopher Confucius bequeathed his own version of it: "To be wronged is nothing, unless you continue to remember it."

From the very first episode when Ted tapes a crooked sign that says 'Believe' onto the locker room wall at AFC Richmond, it seems he is taking us on a journey into self-help territory. Some of his lessons are as obvious as a sign on a wall, but many are more covert. They subliminally creep up on us through plausibly real and difficult situations in which Ted turns negatives into positives, adversity into acceptance, selfish behavior into self-aware behavior. He ensures we understand that it's how we react to difficult situations that makes the difference between coming out smiling or not.

Ted has a wife who wants to divorce him, his soccer team keeps losing, he has a boss who wants to destroy his reputation, and there is a whole stadium of fans calling him offensive names, but Ted is an optimist, a beacon of positivity, a champion of refusing to let circumstances drag him down. Slowly, we see how by repeatedly reacting positively, Ted not only improves his own life, but he also improves the lives of the people around him. Bad things are not going to stop happening to Ted – it would be a dull TV show if they did – but by choosing to react positively each time, he gets to neutralize their negative impact, be at peace with his surroundings, and come out on top.

What makes the show so impactful – aside from the hilarious writing, terrific acting and unexpected plot twists - is that these are psychology textbook ideas, many coming from what has come to be called the Positive Psychology Movement.

Professor Viktor E. Frankl was one of the first psychologists to ask the question: if we approach life with a hopeful frame of mind, as Ted Lasso does, can we shape our own reality? Frankl brought a lot of attention to the idea when he wrote a book called *Man's Search for Meaning* (Beacon Press), published in 1946, in which he chronicled his experience as a prisoner in the Auschwitz concentration camp during World War II.

Like so many there, he was subjected to torture, worked to the brink of death, and watched thousands die around him. But he found himself asking how it was that some people had the strength to survive while others did not. In almost equal circumstances, not everyone fared the same. Why? His conclusion was that human beings have a choice in how we react to the plot twists of our own lives. It seemed to him that those in Auschwitz who had lost faith, meaning, and hope were less likely to survive than those who held onto it. So, is it possible that our reactions to events can influence the outcomes in our lives?

Frankl, along with many psychologists since, believed that we can. And it seems to not be such an unlikely stretch to imagine that perhaps the writers of *Ted Lasso*, Jason Sudeikis among them, do too. "One of the themes is that evil exists — bullies, toxic masculinity, malignant narcissists — and we can't just destroy them. It's about how you deal with those things," Sudeikis has explained in interviews. "That's where the positivity and some of the lessons come in — it's about what we have control over."

Not long after Frankl's *Man's Search for Meaning* came out, another book called *The Power of Positive Thinking: A Practical Guide to Mastering the Problems of Everyday Living* (Simon and Schuster) arrived in American bookstores, going on to become a global best-seller in 1952. It carried a similar strand of thought. Its author, Norman Vincent Peale, believed he could help his readers achieve a permanently optimistic attitude and this would improve their lives. He argued that there was power in picturing yourself succeeding: "The person who sends out positive thoughts activates the world around him positively and draws back to himself positive results." Remind you of anyone? More recently, clinical psychologist Martin Seligman, Ph.D. published a book called *Learned Optimism: How to Change your Mind and Your Life* (Vintage) arguing that people can learn to be optimistic, even if it doesn't come naturally to them.

But optimism and positivity are not Ted's only tricks. He is courteous and respectful, always remembers names, always makes time for the people who are sometimes overlooked– taxi drivers, buskers, and kitman Nate Shelley. "To play someone that was kind-hearted, that didn't swear, be like Teflon toward people's negativity or sarcasm was a hundred percent intentional," Jason Sudeikis has said in interviews.

Generosity is wholly part of who Ted is. His core belief is that all people are worthy, even the ones who are out to trip him up. "You know what you do with tough cookies," Ted tells his boss, Rebecca. "You dip them in milk."

Dozens of papers have been published by The American Psychological Association on how performing acts of generosity and seeing others as worthy can boost our own happiness. Being curious, forgiving, and authentic are believed to have the same effect. Avoiding toxic masculinity, learning to be more open, communicating better, and considering therapy are other ideas that can help us, and each of these turn up in the show as themes too, sometimes so subtly that audiences might not even be aware.

It's as if there are hidden messages to be found in the show if we look for them. And although we all know that Ted Lasso is a fictional character, somehow it doesn't really matter. He is believable enough, human enough, flawed enough, that we notice the value of his example just the same. His kindness is contagious. It's how Ted succeeds in making us want to believe, not just in him, but in ourselves.

So, how can a comedy TV character improve our lives? Incorporating wisdom from psychologists, motivators, and experts in different fields, this unauthorized book is a guide to Ted's life lessons, which are hidden among the laughs of the show. It examines the psychology behind those lessons and what we can all learn from them. It is a book for Tedheads everywhere who want to keep Ted alive in their minds as their very own life coach.

Spoiler alert – plot twists will be revealed.

1

BELIEVE

It's HALF TIME and AFC Richmond is in a tie. The locker room is tense. The boys are jittery because coach Ted Lasso has taken the team's top player, Jamie Tartt, played by Phil Dunster, off the field, and they don't understand why he would do that. Ted doesn't explain. Instead, he delivers a speech as slick as any politician's, and jumps up to slap the sign that he has pasted on the locker room wall, saying 'Believe'.

The message is as clear to the team as it is to us. Believe in yourselves and you can achieve anything.

And since this is a TV show, and the writers can script any outcome they want, it works like a dream. Of course it does. This is TV at its best, intent on pulling us into feel-good drama.

But what about real life? Could believing in ourselves be as simple as slapping a sign? According to psychologists, believing in ourselves is one of the best, sure-fire ways to succeed, and whether it's slapping a sign, telling ourselves out loud in the mirror each morning that 'We're great', or just thinking it, it is the best step towards achieving dreams. Confidence or self-efficacy, a person's belief in their ability to succeed, is one of the most studied topics in psychology. Why? Because our belief in ourselves impacts just about everything in our lives, from how we behave to how we feel, to what goals we choose to set ourselves, and which ones we achieve.

"People's beliefs about their abilities have a profound effect on those abilities," explained the late Professor Albert Bandura, past Professor Emeritus at Stanford University, who is credited as being one of the all-time great psychologists on this subject. "Ability is not a fixed property; there is a huge variability in how you perform," he says.

In other words, if we think we're capable of something, it's possible we really are. But if we don't think we're capable, we won't even try. If we believe we can get our dream job, we'll apply for it, and so naturally there's a chance that we'll get it. If we don't believe we can get it, we won't bother applying and absolutely guarantee that we don't. It's that simple. If we think we'll never be able to learn to drive a car, then we'll never apply for a driving license, guaranteeing that particular outcome. Even the former first lady, Michelle Obama, has weighed in on the subject: "Whether you come from a council estate or a country estate, your success will be determined by your own confidence and fortitude."

But even if the consensus among psychologists is

that confidence in ourselves is more important than our abilities and skillset, how do we find that confidence and self-belief? How do we 'believe in believe,' as Ted tells us we must? Nate, the overlooked kitman who Ted takes under his wing, demonstrates perfectly what it is to have those feelings of inadequacy which haunt many of us.

The night before Richmond plays Everton in the first season, Ted asks kitman Nate, played by Nick Mohammed, if he has any ideas as to what he might say to the team. They've traveled to Liverpool for an away match and the last time the team beat Everton, Elvis Presley had a hit single in the charts. The team needs a win, but Nate won't share his ideas. Why? "Because you won't like my ideas," he tells Ted. "And then you'll hate me. Then you'll fire me. Then I'll have to move back in with my parents, and they'll be ashamed of me."

He's experiencing what psychologists like to call spiraling negative thoughts, which we can all experience from time to time if we let them. We daren't do something because all we can see are risks and the likelihood of failure. But Bandura discovered that people with a weak sense of self-efficacy or lacking in confidence tended to experience these negative thought patterns the most. He found that these people tended to avoid difficult tasks because they imagined that the difficult tasks were beyond their capabilities, and as a result they never really moved forward. They became people who focused more on their personal failings and negative outcomes, rather than seeing opportunities where they might succeed with positive outcomes.

People with a strong sense of self-efficacy, by contrast, tended to be the kind of people who recovered quickly from setbacks and disappointments, they generally liked a challenge and viewed it as something to be mastered. They didn't focus on their failings, only their strengths, and because they had this confidence in themselves, they had a higher chance of success.

In the end, Nate is persuaded to write down his thoughts and strategies about how the team might win the match, and gives them to Ted who embraces them. By being brave enough to take a risk and share his thoughts, Nate succeeds. He doesn't get fired, as he previously imagined. Instead, he gets praised. By believing in his own ideas, he eventually triumphs, and so his confidence grows.

The good news is that anyone can develop a sense of self belief. Bandura managed to prove that self-efficacy is not a trait that some people are born with while others are not. Rather, it's something that can be developed with time, effort, patience, and perseverance.

Nate is a text-book example of what encouragement from others can do for someone. He shows us how confidence can be nurtured, like grass on a soccer field. When we first meet him, he's so over-looked that he's surprised when anyone remembers his name. He gets picked on and bullied in the locker room. But little by little, encouraged by Ted who slowly creates a nurturing atmosphere in the team, we see him dare to speak out, and in so doing, he becomes more confident, finally getting promoted to being an assistant coach.

Bandura argues that social persuasion and social modeling are highly effective tools in building confidence. If someone tells us that we have what it takes, then that can strengthen our self-belief. Also, if we see someone else succeed through dedicated efforts, especially if it's someone just like us, then we can identify with that and imagine ourselves succeeding too. Setting ourselves goals, and persisting until we succeed, is another of his recommendations.

But Bandura also made an important discovery. According to his research, it is much harder to feel confident in our ability to succeed if we're depressed or overwhelmed or tired. Low mood can have a depleting effect on self-belief. People with depression are more likely to give up on goals sooner and be less likely to set themselves goals in the first place.

Since Bandura began his research into the power of self-belief, the subject has exploded into other types of science. In 2015, researchers at Michigan University found that confidence, the colloquial term for self-efficacy, can even create chemical messages in our brain (Nature Neuroscience, January 2016). It is now accepted that when we anticipate success, our brains release a neurotransmitter called dopamine, the chemical messenger that fuels reward and pleasure in the center of the brain.

A generation of motivational books have turned up in bookstores since Bandura brought attention to the subject, almost all of them are committed to the idea that we can learn to believe in ourselves. "To master the art of self-confidence, first master the art of self-awareness and self-love," says Anthony Robbins, one of the best-known life coaches and motivators, author of *Awaken the Giant Within: How to Take Immediate Control of Your Mental, Emotional, Physical and Financial Destiny!* (Simon and Schuster).

Ted is all about that. If Nate is the embodiment of no self-belief at the start, then Ted is poster child for having it. Early into the first series, he retires to the local pub with Coach Beard, played by Brendan Hunt, to open his suggestion box where the team have posted their anonymous ideas. Again and again, the notes call him a wanker, an offensive British term that Ted is not familiar with and has to have explained to him. "You don't want to let them call you that," says Mae, the pub's landlady, played by Annette Badland.

It's the kind of insult that might discourage anyone. But not Ted. He laughs it off. And we get to see in his reaction early on that there is more to Ted than affable Mid-Western charm. We come to understand that perhaps he's been here before, at the receiving end of insults, and he's learned how to let them bounce off him. He chooses his own reaction. We almost get the sense that he was expecting to be insulted and it's all part of his plan. That's when we start to have confidence that he might not know much about soccer, but he knows about winning over and inspiring people. He knows how to not be beaten.

We also see Ted's confidence, that belief in himself, spread to others. By the end of the first series, he has united a team where rivalries once dominated, and he's won everyone round including his boss Rebecca, played by Hannah Waddingham. By the end, she has lost her cynicism. She's no longer bitter. When the team doesn't win the final match, she tells Ted: "Every disadvantage has its advantage," and we see then how Ted's magic has rubbed off on her.

It's all part of the show's charm. And it's a unique charm because the whole show is simply asking the question, just how far can 'Believe' get any one of us?

Eight Tried and Tested Tips which Psychologists Recommend to Boost Self-Confidence.

1. **Exercise.** It doesn't have to be soccer. But it does need to happen. "Your body is like day-old rice. If it ain't warmed up properly, something bad could happen," Ted tells us. Exercise has been proven to enhance mood and influence our minds to positive thought.

2. **Stand tall.** Adopt a posture that makes you feel stronger, because if you feel it, you will be it. Remember the advice Keeley Jones, played by Juno Temple, gave to a nervous Rebecca on the red carpet before the benefit dinner. "Put one foot in front of the other, yeah? And put your hand on your hip and make, like a claw shape."

3. **Step outside your comfort zone and challenge yourself.** As Ted says: "Takin' on a challenge is a lot like riding a horse. If you're comfortable while you're doin' it, you're probably doin' it wrong."

4. **Encourage yourself. Words matter.** Ted has 'Believe' signs pasted all over his house, including on the bathroom mirror so he sees it first thing in the morning and last thing at night when he rationalizes being too tired to floss.

5. **Practice gratitude.** Every time anyone does or says something helpful, Ted says: "I appreciate you." It's an intentional misuse of the phrase 'I appreciate it,' and it works especially well because it emphasizes that we should appreciate the people in our lives, as much as the things they do for us. Boosting others boosts our own confidence.

6. **Practice self-love.** "Go easy on yourself," Ted tells Roy Kent, played by Brett Goldstein. "You had a bad day. Big Whoop. You beating yourself up is like Woody Allen playing clarinet, I won't hear it."

7. **Visualize goals and work hard:** "As the man once said, the harder you work, the luckier you get."

8. **Take an interest in others and everything around you.** "We can't really be good partners unless we get to know each other, right?" Ted tells Rebecca. When you get to know people, you become more empathetic and relate better with them, which in turn, boosts confidence.

2

BE SUCCESSFUL

IT'S RIGHT THERE from the very start. A secret nod. Blink and you might miss it. When Ted and Coach Beard settle into their new office at AFC Richmond, we watch them rearrange the furniture, turning their desks to face each other; pinning posters of their sporting heroes to the walls, and then finally, a framed picture of a triangle is set reverently in position. The camera lingers only briefly on it, but it's significant. The triangle is an autographed copy of an image from *John Wooden's Pyramid of Success*.

Jason Sudeikis who, besides playing Ted, co-created the show with Brendan Hunt, Joe Kelly and Bill Lawrence, has said many times that he drew inspiration for Ted from both his own high school coach and also John Wooden, a real-life coach, who made sporting history for leading UCLA's men's basketball teams to ten NCAA championships in twelve years.

Wooden is significant because he was more than just a coach, he was a motivator beyond the sports field; some might have even called him a life-coach or a philosopher. "I found the writings and philosophies of John Wooden, the great UCLA college basketball coach to be profound," Sudeikis has said in interviews. "His philosophies were things I used to teach when I was coaching improv."

More than simply being famous for his sporting success, Wooden came to be celebrated everywhere for his philosophies on life. He became famous for challenging the idea of what defines success. He believed that it was not about winning or losing, rather about the effort it took in trying to be the best version of yourself that you could possibly be. "Success is peace of mind which is a direct result of self-satisfaction in knowing you made the effort to become the best you are capable of becoming," Wooden is renowned for saying in 1948.

That sentiment is echoed in Ted's words when he tells journalist, Trent Crimm of The Independent, played by James Lance, who is writing a profile about him: "For me, success is not about the wins and losses. It's about helping these young fellas be the best versions of themselves on and off the field." Crimm is so astonished by the idea that a coach might care less about the team winning than about the personal development of his players that he asks Ted to repeat himself. Yes, he did hear him correctly.

Like Wooden, Jason Sudeikis has said in interviews that he also tries to apply those principles and philosophies to his own life. Long before *Ted Lasso* was created,

Sudeikis taught improv comedy and would always quote John Wooden, quizzing actors on the importance of industriousness and enthusiasm. His own school basketball coach had used *The Pyramid of Success*, Wooden's book, as a guide and inspiration when Sudeikis was young.

Wooden began writing down his ideas about what success might mean in 1934 when he was a 24-year-old high school coach in Dayton, Kentucky. He approached the game from a philosophical perspective, reaching the conclusion that success wasn't about the final score. He argued that if you can become a good person in your own life, then you stand the best chance of becoming a good player on the team and this, in turn, may lead to wins, but that is not necessarily the main goal. "The best way to improve the team is to improve ourselves," he is famous for saying, insisting that success was about the journey of the game.

It was a revolutionary idea in sports. But Wooden's views on success are not the only ones to be found in the show. Tucked neatly into the second season, we catch Coach Beard reading Matthew Syed's *The Greatest: What Sport Teaches Us About Achieving Success* (John Murray). Syed was the English number one table tennis player for many years and is now a motivational leader, who argues in his books and lectures that the key to success is a positive attitude to failure. We cannot grow unless we are prepared to learn from our mistakes, according to Syed. "Above all, we need to understand that anyone who has achieved anything impressive has gone through multiple stages of imperfection," he says.

In other words, could it be that if we strive to be our best selves, if we learn from our mistakes, then we are already being successful? "You all played a heck of a game. You might not have won, but you all succeeded," Ted tells his team after a loss.

But just as Wooden was, Ted gets challenged. Towards the end of the first season, team captain Roy Kent, played by Brett Goldstein, has become too old and slow for the game. Ted is under pressure to take him off the field, but Ted says it would be humiliating for Roy to be benched. He tells Coach Beard in The Crown and Anchor, their local pub, that's not how he likes to measure success. Beard disagrees.

Wooden faced similar pressures because sometimes it's hard to argue you are succeeding if you lose a game. But he never gave up on the ideal, and his record of consecutive wins speaks for itself.

Wooden's *Pyramid of Success* is essentially a 15 building-block framework of successful behaviors, in which each block represents a human trait or value, which when placed in line with the others, leads to an apex of competitive greatness that can be applied to anything in life. At its base Wooden recommends individuals to seek industriousness, friendship, loyalty, co-operation, and enthusiasm. On top, come self-control, alertness, initiative, intentness, condition, skill, team spirit, poise, confidence, and finally competitive greatness. Holding the pyramid together are ten other qualities, which Wooden calls the mortar: ambition, honesty, integrity, faith, patience, sincerity, reliability, fight, resourcefulness, and adaptability.

Because *The Pyramid of Success* has no specific reference to basketball or any sport at all, it remains a useful leadership tool, regarded as a road map for anyone looking to achieve success. It is still regularly used in schools and corporations. Given the success of the show – the first season making television history at the *Primetime Emmy Awards* in 2021 as the most nominated freshman comedy in history – it's almost spooky that a show that showcased Wooden's ideals achieved so much itself.

The creation of *Ted Lasso* began in 2013 as a commercial. He was a promotional character for NBC, which had acquired the TV rights to the UK's Premier League, dreamed up by Sudeikis and Brendan Hunt. The idea was that a brief *Saturday Night Live* style sketch about an ignorant US football coach teaching English soccer, a sport he knows nothing about, in a country he's never been to before, would inspire American interest in the game. As a commercial, it went down well. People thought Ted was funny, and that might have been the end of him, except that Jason Sudeikis kept thinking.

Sudeikis felt there was a show to be made still. But he wanted Ted's character to be different from the coach in the commercial. He didn't want Ted to simply be ignorant. He wanted him to be curious and kind too. "A thing I have felt for a long time is that the worst version of 'a human man' is a guy who is ignorant but arrogant," Sudeikis explains. "And so, we wanted to play a guy that was ignorant, yes, but also curious – and that's a subtle touch. We wanted to make a show that didn't rely on cynicism. It was about what we didn't want to do… And time and again we came back to kindness and empathy."

And so Ted was born, a fish out of water still. But not an arrogant one. He was someone who incorporated all those characteristics and traits that John Wooden had considered so carefully nearly a hundred years before – sincerity, honesty, reliability, industriousness, confidence - but most importantly, he was someone who wanted to encourage everyone around him to adopt those traits too.

And just in case audiences might miss that point, it's up there on the wall of Ted's office in a frame to remind us.

Wooden's Ideals

www.coachwooden.com

Industriousness

Friendship

Loyalty

Self-Control

Alertness

Initiative

Intentness

Condition

Skill

Team Spirit

Poise

Confidence

Competitive Greatness

3

BE CURIOUS

Ask any *Ted Lasso* fan, or Tedhead as they have come to be called, to describe a scene that best encapsulates what Ted represents, and most likely they'll hum and haw a while because there's a lot of choice. But eventually they will remember the moment when Ted takes on Rebecca's cheating ex-husband, Rupert Mannion, played by Anthony Head, in a game of darts in The Crown and Anchor. It's a moment that seems to demonstrate, more than any other, what the show is all about - integrity triumphing over dishonesty, decency over immorality, underdogs winning, but on their own terms.

Rupert is arrogant and contemptuous of Ted. He's just bought shares in the soccer club, which under the terms of his divorce settlement with Rebecca he is not allowed to do. He has sneakily bought them in his fian-cée's name, delivering two brutal blows to Rebecca – not only the news that he plans to marry again, but also that he'll be turning up in the owner's box each week. He's rich. He's powerful. He's intent on making his ex-wife's life a misery.

Like a gallant knight to the rescue in a medieval joust, Ted embarks on a game of darts with Rupert, setting the stakes of the game. If Rupert wins, Ted will allow Rupert to pick the starting lineup for the last two soccer games of the season. If Ted wins, Rupert won't go anywhere near the owner's box for as long as Rebecca is still in charge. "Are you sure you know what you're doing, Ted?" we want to yell at our TV screens when Rupert produces some professional darts from his pocket.

A crowd gathers. Suspense mounts. Especially when at first, it looks as if Ted doesn't even know how to play the game. For a simple game of darts, it's strikingly compelling. Finally, Ted needs two triple twenties and a bullseye to win, which seems unlikely. But then Ted begins a soliloquy as astute as anything ever written by Shakespeare: "Guys have underestimated me my entire life, and for years, I never understood why," he says matter-of-factly, as he takes aim. "It used to bother me. But then one day I was driving my little boy to school, and I saw this quote by Walt Whitman painted on a wall there, it said: 'Be curious, not judgmental'. I like that."

Ted hits his first twenty, and we realize he does know how to play darts after all. Now the tension really builds. But Ted is untroubled. Cool as the unlikely superhero we know he is, his soliloquy continues, explaining that in that moment he'd had a revelation. "All those fellas who belittled me, they weren't curious," he says, eyeing the dartboard. "They thought they had everything figured out, so they judged everything, and they judged everyone, and I realized that their underestimating of me, of who I was, had nothing to do with it...."

He hits his second twenty; and we lean in even closer. "Because if they were curious, they would have asked questions. Questions like 'Have you played a lot of darts, Ted?' To which I would have answered 'Yes, Sir. Every Sunday afternoon at a sports bar with my dad from age ten to sixteen when he passed away'."

Ted hits his bullseye and wins, delivering a glorious life lesson not only to Rupert, but to all of us, which is that curiosity can make us better individuals.

Psychologists believe that one of the greatest benefits of being curious is that it not only gives us the power of knowledge, but it also leads to emotional well-being. Study after study has found that being curious makes us more content, strengthens our relationships, makes us more creative, it leads to higher levels of achievement, and it even helps us survive.

"The urge to explore and seek novelty helps us remain vigilant and gain knowledge about our constantly changing environment, which may be why our brains evolved to release dopamine and other feel-good chemicals when we encounter new things," explains Emily Campbell, Ph.D., Research Associate at the Greater Good Science Center at the University of California, Berkeley. "Research has shown curiosity to be associated with higher levels of positive emotions, lower levels of anxiety, more satisfaction with life."

Being judgmental of others, on the other hand, tends to have the oppositive effect. Ted talks specifically of people who wanted to belittle him. We've all encountered people like that. At their most extreme, we'd probably call them bullies. But as he explains so eloquently, other people's judgment of us has nothing to do with who we are, but everything to do with who *they* are. Those who judge others, tend to draw from their own feelings and sense of insecurity. They often suffer from low self-esteem themselves, so they target others to feel better about themselves.

How to avoid becoming one of those super-critical, judgmental types? Be curious, instead. Or, have empathy which psychologists regard as a closely linked trait. "For me, the core of empathy is curiosity," explains Jodi Halpern, MD. Ph.D., a psychiatrist and bioethics professor at the University of California, Berkeley. "What is another person's life actually like in its particulars?" In other words, when we are curious about others and talk to people, we become better able to understand them, which is what empathy is all about.

We might see a woman in a department store, for example, who is struggling to control her children while waiting in line at the check-out. The baby in the stroller is crying, the two older kids are running everywhere. The woman keeps looking at her phone. Anyone in a judgmental frame of mind, standing next to her, might find themselves asking: 'Why aren't her kids in school?', 'Why doesn't she shut the baby up?', 'Why's she on her phone?' 'Why doesn't she control her children?' Within minutes, we are making judgments about the woman's parenting skills, perhaps labeling her with the most uncharitable of titles, a bad mother. It's easily done.

But what would Ted do if he was standing next to her in line? He'd talk to her, of course. He'd be inventing a game to play with the kids, handing them a couple of his little green army men. But in talking to her, he might learn that the woman's husband had abandoned her for another woman this morning and she's looking at her phone because she's waiting to hear back from a lawyer. He might also learn that school is closed for the day and the woman had to go to the mall because her daughter needs new basketball shoes for a game tomorrow. She's not a bad mother. She's a good mother in stressed circumstances. If we are curious about others, we get to stand in their shoes a moment and learn that any assumptions we might make about that person are probably wrong.

Through the first season, Jamie is a bully. He's arrogant and unkind. But Ted is patient with him. He remains kind, even in the most testing of circumstances, refusing to quit on him, remaining curious about him. Even asking Keeley, his girlfriend at the time, played by Juno Temple, what's the best way to get through to him? Ted knows there will be a reason why Jamie is the way that he is. And there is, which we come to see in the second season, with Ted carefully showing us that curiosity is a better, kinder path than judging others too quickly.

The term empathy was first introduced in 1909 by a

British born psychologist Edward B. Titchener, studying at Cornell University. He used it to describe the capacity of human beings to be in tune with another's emotions. Today psychologists and neuroscientists are fascinated by the subject because it challenges the idea that humans are entirely self-interested beings. Rather than fitting into a 'survival of the fittest' theory, as Charles Darwin speculated, it suggests that human beings are hotwired for cooperation and mutual aid. Which might seem a long way off from a TV show about a soccer coach winning a darts match, except that mutual aid and cooperation, are what Ted is all about. They build teams and ultimately help him.

Remember how down in the dumps Sam, played by Toheeb Jimoh, was, early on in the first season? Ted is curious why and asks the other team members what they think the problem is. He discovers that Sam is homesick, so he organizes a collection among the team, buys Sam some birthday gifts, makes him feel he has support away from home, and Sam is motivated once more. According to a 2021 *Forbes* study, 86% of the people they interviewed reported that they were able to navigate the demands of their work and life better when their leaders and managers were more empathetic. Curiosity does not kill the cat; it strengthens the team.

It's why empathy (curiosity in disguise) has become a buzz word in business. It's why corporations and HR leaders send managers on empathy training courses. A decade ago, that might have been laughed at. But it is now understood that if leaders are curious about others, if they can understand the emotions and stories of others and learn to be good listeners, seeing things from someone else's point of view, then the workplace becomes more productive and successful. "In the not-too-distant past, discussing empathy as a required characteristic of a leader would have been a rarity," says Mary Ludden Ph.D., teaching professor at Northeastern's College of Professional Studies. "But the truth of the matter is that all of us are seeking deeper connections not only in our personal lives, but from our professional colleagues as well. Our ability to connect with each other on all levels of our consciousness will differentiate great leaders from being good managers."

Glassdoor, the recruitment specialists, were among the first to recognize the empathy in leadership trend. Late in 2020, they published a list of the top-performing CEOs in the US and UK, based on employee reviews. The common traits that put these CEOs on the list was their willingness to listen, to prioritize employee wellbeing, offer flexible working arrangements and maintain clear communication. In essence, it was their ability to be empathetic that put them on top.

Right from the start of the first season, when Ted and Coach Beard are met at Heathrow by a taxi service, we see Ted's curiosity in others. Within minutes, he knows the name of taxi-driver Ollie, played by Jimmy Akingbola, and he is asking him questions, getting along so well that Ted is invited to Ollie's father-in-law's Indian restaurant, where he takes Trent Crimm in a later episode. That curiosity is why, even before he arrives at AFC Richmond, we're already rooting for him, already suspecting that he's going to make a great coach, no matter what.

Cam Cole, the one-man-band busker who plays himself, gets Ted's undivided attention too on the street corner outside his house, which turns out to be useful when Robbie Williams is a no-show for Rebecca's benefit dinner, and she needs a band. "You do not wanna judge this book by its cover," Ted tells Rebecca when she looks skeptically at Cam in his shabby clothes.

Of course, Cam turns out to be a terrific musician. And that's the point – judging books by covers doesn't help any of us. Each time Ted is curious about others, we see how happy the connections make him, how they enhance his life. Being curious, as he tells Rupert Mannion, is the antidote to being judgmental.

How We Can Be More Empathetic and Less Judgmental.

1. Put away your phone and start conversations with strangers. Go beyond small talk, ask someone about his or her life. Studies have shown that people who ask questions of others and demonstrate real curiosity are perceived as being warmer individuals.

2. We are all judgmental. We form conclusions about people all the time. But catching ourselves doing it, and trying to be actively curious instead, will serve us better.

3. Read books. The more we learn about others, the more we will understand that negative judgments are usually unwarranted.

4. Don't make assumptions about people based on what your life is like. Other people's lives might not be as privileged as yours. Always challenge prejudice.

5. Model empathy for children. Empathy can be learned.

6. Listen to others. Even if you disagree, don't interrupt. Use body language to show you are actively listening.

4

BE OPTIMISTIC

IT'S THE FINAL episode of the first season and AFC Richmond are up against Manchester City, a champion team they must beat or they'll be relegated. "It's hopeless," says Nate, who is in Ted's living room with Coach Beard trying to come up with a strategy for the team to win. Coach Beard isn't much help either. "You are both so damn pessimistic," Ted says to them, diving into a theme which courses through the show's veins.

We know Ted is a relentless optimist. We've been watching it play out in every episode. It's why we love him. Now, his optimism seems to come under threat, perhaps deliberately, to underscore to us the difference between pessimism and optimism. "I hate to say this, but your football club might have been better off with a real soccer coach," he tells Rebecca.

What? This can't be the Ted that we know! "Don't do

that to us, Ted!" we call out to him from our sofas. "We, your adoring audience, believe in you. We've come to see the value of optimism. You can't possibly give up now."

Fortunately, Rebecca is there to say it for us, transformed over the season, from bitter to encouraging, demonstrating neatly the value of optimism. "Every disadvantage has an advantage," she tells him.

"Thank you, Rebecca," we yell once more at our screens.

It does the trick. In the locker room before the big match, Ted delivers the message we've all been waiting for, the one the team needs to hear, and the one we all need to hear too: "You all got a phrase here that I ain't crazy about. 'It's the hope that kills you'." Ted scratches his chin earnestly. "I disagree. I think it's the lack of hope that comes to get you. I believe in hope. I believe in believe."

And that's a question we can all ask ourselves. Do we believe in believe? Do we imagine good outcomes or bad? Do we usually see a way forward or only setbacks? And if we experience setbacks, are we able to see them as temporary, one-time only events, or do we imagine that they'll last forever, and we'll never get beyond them?

How we approach life, with optimism or pessimism, can influence how well we do. Study after study has proved this. Optimists have been found to be higher achievers. They also have better overall health, live longer, have better job satisfaction, demonstrate greater resilience, and have even been proven to have lower rates of cancer. What's not to love? Pessimists, on the other hand, do not fare so well. They give up more easily, tend to suffer from depression, mental health problems, and have even been found to be more likely to get sick.

So, which do we want to be?

The good news is that it's a choice. Our mindset is not carved in stone. According to psychologists, optimism can be a deliberate, intentional choice, and we can teach ourselves strategies to make that happen. It's called 'Learned Optimism', a phrase coined by psychologist Martin E.P. Seligman, Ph.D., who is often credited as being the father of the Positive Psychology Movement. "Pessimists can, in fact, learn to be optimists," explains Seligman, Professor of Psychology at the University of Pennsylvania, past president of the American Psychological Association, and motivational expert.

For him, optimism is not the simple seeing a glass half-full versus half empty idea that is frequently used to define optimism. "Rather, it consists of the way that you think about setbacks and the way you think about victories," he explains. "The optimistic person when they have a setback believes that its temporary, they think 'I can change it, it's just this situation'. The pessimistic person who experiences a setback believes it's going to last forever and that it's going to undermine everything they do."

Seligman began his research, looking at what he called 'learned helplessness', which means giving up when you believe that nothing you do will make any difference. He carried out an experiment with two dogs placed in separate boxes that produced small electric shocks. One dog managed to escape the box, but the other dog could not escape no matter what he did. He kept getting electric shocks. In other words, he experienced setbacks.

Those same dogs were then put in two different boxes that they could both escape from easily. The dog that had learned that he could get out of the box before, got out straight away. The other dog remembered what had happened before, and had now come to believe that no matter what he did there was nothing he could do to escape, so he just lay down. He didn't even try to escape. Seligman believes that some people who repeatedly experience setbacks in the same way can learn to be helpless. If we think we can't do something, it becomes a self-fulfilling prophecy.

When AFC Richmond play Everton in an away game in Liverpool, the team are depressed because every time they've played Everton for the last sixty years, they've lost. Like the dog in Seligman's box who has given up, they have convinced themselves that it won't matter how they play, they are sure to suffer humiliation because they have lost so many times before, stretching back to when Elvis Presley was number one in the charts. In other words, they have learned to be helpless. But under Ted's guidance, and some home truths from Nate, they are encouraged to change their thinking. They have to forget about what has gone before. They have to learn to be optimistic. As a result, demonstrating the point neatly, they win.

Seligman spent years studying the differences between optimists and pessimists, asking thousands of people thousands of questions. He reached the conclusion that the big difference between them seemed to be in how they explained events that had happened in their lives. Pessimists tended to view bad times as permanent and unchangeable. They had tried something before, and it hadn't worked out, so they argued to themselves: 'Why try again?' They tended to personalize bad outcomes too. They blamed themselves, imagining that the failure or setback must have been their fault, or there was something wrong with them, when that might not have been the case at all. But they convinced themselves of this so well, they decided to give up. Pessimists also saw setbacks as pervasive. In other words, if they failed at one thing, they imagined they would fail at everything. They took one failure or set back and allowed it to influence everything else, imagining they must be useless at everything. So once again, they gave up, and nothing guarantees failure better than not trying in the first place. "The depressive's habit of thinking that the future is bleak, the present unbearable, the past filled with defeat, and the self without the ability to improve matters creates the low mood, the lack of zest, and the somatic symptoms of depression," Seligman explains.

The optimists who Seligman interviewed didn't see bad times as permanent at all. They saw them as blips, small moments to forget about like Ted's goldfish moment. Just because they tried something, and it hadn't worked out, so what? It wasn't going to stop them trying again. It wasn't going to stop them working out another route. As a result, they bounced back.

Optimists didn't personalize any failures either. If an unfavorable outcome occurred, they imagined it must be because of outside influences. It wasn't anything to do with their abilities. They might blame it on the weather, or luck, or something else that might have happened spoiling their chances. It certainly wasn't their fault. They also refused to let that one particular failure or setback become pervasive. In other words, they didn't let one setback influence their beliefs in their abilities in other areas. Just because they experienced a setback in one area, didn't mean they weren't fantastic at others. And so, the optimists tended to do better because they kept trying.

Staring hard at all his research, Seligman's big lightbulb moment arrived: if human beings can learn to be helpless, does that mean they can learn to be optimistic too? And the answer, a resounding 'Yes', was a big moment in the history of psychology because it opened up the possibility that people who have suffered mental health issues and trauma could learn to adjust their worldview, and with training, learn to focus on being happy and optimistic again.

Seligman's further research also helped him understand that you could teach optimism skills to children. His book, *The Optimistic Child: A Proven Program to Safeguard Children Against Depression and Build Lifelong Resilience* (Houghton Mifflin) became a best seller. "Feelings of self-esteem in particular, and happiness in general, develop as side effects — of mastering challenges, working successfully, overcoming frustration and boredom, and winning," Seligman explains. "The feeling of self-esteem is a byproduct of doing well. Once a child's self-esteem is in place, it kindles further success. Tasks flow more seamlessly, troubles bounce off."

The point is we all experience setbacks at one time or another. They are part of life. Not even Ted is exempt. The issue is how we cope with them. When Ted faces setbacks - an entire stadium calling him a wanker, lost matches, cruel commentaries from sports writers, sarcasm, criticism - he doesn't give up. He's like Teflon, impervious to the castigation, rolling with the punches. Even when Ted says goodbye to his wife Michelle, played by Andrea Andrews, both standing in the rain with tears falling down their cheeks because Michelle wants to separate, we know Ted's going to be alright. "You don't have to keep trying anymore," he tells her. "I'm gonna be alright." As painful as it is for him, he wants her to know he's going to be fine.

Long before Martin Seligman began his studies into optimism, another psychologist was curious about the subject too. This time the setback was arguable the biggest that any human could ever face, and he was facing it personally. Victor E. Frankl was a well-regarded psychologist living in Vienna, Austria, when he was imprisoned by the Nazis and sent to Auschwitz concentration camp in 1942, along with his family. Frankl had already been working on a psychology theory which he called logotherapy, the idea that life can hold meaning regardless of one's circumstance. At Auschwitz, after losing his family and living in the worst circumstance possible – starved, beaten, tortured, living in freezing temperatures - he found he had the opportunity to put his theory to the test personally.

He was also able to witness how others dealt with the horror of concentration camp life and noticed two types of prisoners: those who seemed to have lost all hope, and those who held onto it, seeing their circumstances as challenges to be overcome. Those who kept hoping and looking for a meaning and purpose in life seemed to fare better. Those who lost all sense of purpose, were the ones more likely to get sick and die. Frankl believed he survived because he kept thinking about his work, imagining the lectures he would give on this subject when he was free again.

There were many take-aways from Frankl's experiences which he wrote in his extraordinary best-seller, *Man's Search for Meaning* (Beacon Press) published in English in 1959,, but he was perhaps the first to argue with solid proof that we always have a choice in how we approach circumstances. "Everything can be taken from a man but one thing: the last of the human freedoms – to choose one's attitude in any given set of circumstances, to choose one's own way."

It seems that might be Jason Sudeikis' personal philosophy too. Shortly after the first season of *Ted Lasso* aired, he and his partner Olivia Wilde, with whom he has two children, separated. He has said it was a difficult experience in many press interviews, but like Ted, he seemed to recognize that he had a choice in how he reacted. "I think if you have the opportunity to hit a rock bottom, however you define that, you can become 412 bones or you can land like an Avenger," he explained in one interview. "I personally have chosen to land like an Avenger. It doesn't mean when you blast back up, you're not going to run into a bunch of shit and have to fight things to get back to the heights that you were at, but I'd take that over 412 bones anytime."

There will always be external forces working against us – jobs we want but don't get, rain that spoils picnics, car crashes, over-drafts, unrequited love, lost loves, lost soccer matches – the key to coming out on top is how we react to them, because although we cannot control the external forces, we can control our responses and attitudes to them. Even in a concentration camp with no physical freedom, Frankl still found freedom in how he thought and in how he chose his attitude. That choice is what can influence how well, and sometimes if, we survive. "When we are no longer able to change a situation, we are challenged to change ourselves," he wrote.

Or, in Ted's words: "You say 'impossible', but all I hear is 'I'm possible'."

How To Be More Optimistic.

1. Think about a situation that was difficult for you.
2. Did you think 'I'm useless' as a result?
3. Did it stop you trying again?
4. Now think of a situation where you were successful and kept going.
5. Can you see how a setback might stop you when it shouldn't?
6. Read: *Learned Optimism: How to Change Your Mind and Your Life*, by Martin E.P. Seligman, Ph.D.

5

BE A DO-GOODER

HALFWAY THROUGH THE second season, the show unexpectedly seems to take a break from running plot lines that move the season forward. Jamie Tartt is happy to be back on the team. Roy and Keeley (who broke up with Jamie and later found romance with Roy) are together. Rebecca has accepted being single. There is no note of discord or tension anywhere. And it's Christmas! In August! (Yup, that's when the show aired). Which might seem a bit odd, until you realize that this episode seems to exist solely for the purpose of celebrating good deeds. And it's as warm and fuzzy as a Santa suit.

After Ted's first FaceTime Christmas with his son ends, he pours himself a lonely, solo whiskey, and sits back to watch Jimmy Stewart contemplate ending it all in *It's a Wonderful Life* on TV. Everything points to it being a cold, sad Christmas for Ted. But suddenly

Rebecca is outside his window telling him to come join her. She remembers what her first Christmas alone after divorce was like, and takes him knocking on doors to deliver Christmas gifts to kids who sent Santa letters, reminding us that the most self-serving thing that any of us can ever do is always to help someone else.

Meanwhile the Higgins family, who always open their house to any of AFC Richmond's players far from their families at Christmas, are inundated. Player after player turns up on their doorstep and we catch Leslie and Julie Higgins, played by Jeremy Swift and Mary Roscoe, wondering how they will ever fit so many – nearly a full football team - into their tiny house that is already stretched to bursting with their five boys. But no-one gets turned away. Not on *Ted Lasso*. Not on a Christmas special that spills over with tidings of generosity and Higgins toasting "The family we're born with, and the family we make along the way." Besides, a squashed, filled-to-the-rafters Christmas makes the Higgins family happy.

There's no getting away from this sugar-and-spice yuletide message. Doing good deeds makes us feel good about ourselves. It's a well-studied, scientific fact that by helping others, we help ourselves because it makes us forget about ourselves and so our burdens are lifted.

The term altruism was invented by the French sociologist and philosopher Auguste Comte in the nineteenth century. It is derived from the Latin word, *alteri*, meaning 'to others', and refers to the practice of concern for other human beings or animals. It's another major topic for psychologists because like empathy, altruism challenges the idea that human beings are wired to be selfish and are only out for their own advancement. Many studies have even been able to show that by performing acts of altruism, human beings seem to experience happiness and greater satisfaction in life, and overall wellness. Which seems to confuse the whole issue, because if that's the case, maybe we're all selfish at heart anyway. Who knows? Like Ted says "If that's a joke, I love it. If not, I cannot wait to unpack that."

But in the meantime, studies continue to flood in showing that doing good deeds, or volunteerism as psychologists call it, makes us feel good about ourselves and contributes so effectively to better health, it can even lengthen our life expectancy. A study published by the American Psychological Association in 2013 found that adults aged over 50 who volunteered for four hours a week were 40% less likely than non-volunteers to develop high blood pressure four years later.

Even more extraordinary was an experiment carried out by Dr. Liz Dunn, professor in the Department of Psychology at the University of British Columbia and co-author of *Happy Money: The Science of Happier Spending* (Simon and Schuster). She gave a group of people ten dollars and instructed them that they could keep the money or give any amount of it away. "What we found, consistent with all our past research, was that the more money people gave away, the happier they felt. Conversely though, the more money people kept for themselves, the more shame they experienced. And the more shame people felt, the more we saw their cortisol levels rise, which is important because cortisol is thought to explain some of the links that we've seen between stress and disease."

Researchers at the University of Buffalo conducted similar research following a large group of people over a five-year period, and found that those who volunteered reported less stress and, over time, had a reduced mortality rate. So too a group of mothers who were followed over a thirty-year period for another study published in the American Journal of Sociology. It found that of those who volunteered on a regular basis, only 36% experienced a major illness, while 52% of those who did not belong to a volunteer organization did.

Volunteering is like the superfood of the Positive Psychology world, according to Dawn Carr, MGS, Ph.D., writing in *Psychology Today (Five Reasons Why You Should Volunteer. March 2014)*. "Later in life, volunteering is even more beneficial for one's health than exercising and eating well," she says. "Older people who volunteer remain physically functional longer, have more robust psychological well-being, and live longer.

"Although it is not well understood why volunteering has such a profound health benefit, a key factor is assumed to be that volunteering serves to express and facilitate opportunities to carry out one's sense of purpose."

Which ties in with what Viktor E. Frankl was saying in *Man's Search for Meaning*. If we can find a meaning to our lives, a sense of purpose, then we're on a good path to our own survival. Volunteering then, is something that we all need to do. So, it shouldn't really be surprising that doing good deeds found its way into the show. It's all part of the vibe.

Volunteering, it turns out, is also as much a part of who Jason Sudeikis is in real life as it is a part of who Ted is. For more than a decade, the actor and writer has hosted and continues to host "The Big Slick," a fun packed fund-raising weekend with other celebrities from Kansas City, raising more than $13 million for the local Children's Mercy Hospital. Does that remind you of the gala dinner benefitting underprivileged children, hosted by Rebecca in the first season? Of course it does.

Sudeikis also continues to host the benefit concert "Thundergong!" in Kansas City, for the Steps of Faith Foundation which helps provide prosthetic legs and arms to those in need. Then there was the "Red Nose Day Special," a UK telethon raising funds for charity; appearances on the NBA All-Star basketball celebrity team; and cooler still, Ted's delivery of gifts for children with Rebecca in the Christmas episode is based on Sudeikis's experience with the real-life charity, "Letters to Santa," run by Poverty Alleviation Charities, for whom he helped raise funds in Chicago.

Sudeikis is clearly someone who's got a heart. All of which leads to the question: how much of an overlap is there between Jason Sudeikis and Ted? At the premiere of the show's second season, Sudeikis showed up in a 'Jadon & Marcus & Bukayo' shirt in support of the England soccer players who had experienced racist abuses following the team's Euro 2020 final loss. If ever there was a

Ted move, that would be it. So, are the two the same? It seems reasonable to consider.

Like Ted, Daniel Jason Sudeikis grew up in Kansas, home of Ted's cheerful twang. He was born in Fairfax, Virginia, in 1975, but moved to Kansas early. His mom was a travel agent, his dad was a business executive, and he has two younger sisters. He attended Shawnee Mission West High School and has often said that the coach of his school team, Donnie Campbell, was one of his inspirations for Ted, alongside his father. "That's where the mustache comes from and him being real loquacious," he says. But Sudeikis liked improv comedy as much as he did sport and started performing at ComedySportz in Kansas City. Gigs in Chicago and Las Vegas followed when he became part of The Second City Touring Company.

Humor and wit mattered to him. Spotted as a rising talent, he was drafted into *Saturday Night Live (SNL)* in 2003, where he worked first as a writer before becoming one of its stars. Eight further years on *SNL*, as well as parts in TV shows like *It's Always Sunny in Philadelphia*, roles in films like *We're the Millers* and *Horrible Bosses*, and Jason Sudeikis was an established working comedy actor. But he was never quite the breakthrough star until *Ted Lasso* made him one at 45 years old in 2020. There is a poster in Ted's office in the show that reads: 'Gradarius Firmus Victoria', Slow and Steady Wins the Race. The message could be equally applied to Sudeikis's career.

But it seems that an ambitious career path was not Sudeikis's sole motivation. His friendships mattered greatly. He met Brendan Hunt while they were working in improv together in Chicago back in the nineties. From that friendship, a collaborative writing partnership was born. They like to tell the story that while they were in Amsterdam with their improv troupe, Boom Chicago, they'd play the FIFA video game together in the dressing room, Hunt as Manchester United and Sudeikis as Arsenal, and that became the inspiration for their first version of Ted, created for the NBC promo ad, with Hunt appearing in the commercial alongside. Joe Kelly, the show's other co-creator, was another old friend from Sudeikis's *SNL* days.

Sudeikis has always described Ted as the best version of himself. "He's like me after two beers on an empty stomach on a bright sunny day." Others are more emphatic about it. Marcus Mumford, another old friend, and composer of the music on the show, says "He is quite like Ted in lots of ways. He has a sort of burning optimism, but also a vulnerability." Brendan Hunt describes him as having "an easygoing confidence. And it's easy to hang with a guy like that."

But whether Sudeikis is or isn't Ted, there has never been any doubt about the intention behind Ted's creation. "Be the change you wish to see in the world," Sudeikis has said, quoting the political and spiritual leader Mahatma Gandi in interviews, adding "Create the world where being nice, being uncynical, being egoless, being empathetic and promoting forgiveness is not something that is weak and happens without consequences."

Which explains why an episode about good deeds was always destined to turn up in the show.

Reasons to Volunteer

1. It connects you to others, providing opportunities for friendships.
2. It increases your social and relationship skills.
3. It counteracts the effects of stress, anger, anxiety, and depression.
4. It increases self-confidence.
5. It provides a sense of purpose.
6. It helps you stay physically healthy.
7. It can advance your career.
8. It leads to happiness.

6

BE OPEN TO THERAPY

THERAPY? WHY PAY someone to do for you what a friend should do for free, Ted asks Rebecca, at the start of the second season, both sitting on the sofa in her office.

"That's why you have friends," she agrees. "To burden them with your issues and anxieties, right?"

Well, let's consider that. The writers of the show certainly have.

In this season, the characters get more complicated and real. They become even more like us. And there's the arrival of sports therapist, Dr. Sharon Fieldstone, played by Sarah Niles, who is making Ted jumpy. "Every time I look round, she seems to be getting closer," Ted says nervously. Slowly, we come to understand that Ted's sunny approach to life might be a coping mechanism for something bad that happened to him. We see him get debilitating panic attacks. We see him vulnerable, and realize that underneath that charming, mustachioed façade, something's up.

But he's not owning up to it. We're in murkier terrain now with only one thing that's crystal clear: he's absolutely set against therapy. He appears to be frightened by it. "You don't know me. We don't have history and yet you just expect me to spill my guts about all the gory details of my life," he tells Dr. Sharon, before storming out of her office, showing us a hostile side to Ted that we haven't seen before. Several times he bolts from her office. It's a response that many of us might sympathize with because sometimes therapy can be scary. And that's the big red flag waving to us on our sofas, telling us what the overarching theme of this season is. Seeking help and being open about our problems takes courage, but therapy can make a difference.

Fighting our interior battles is something that plagues all of us. No one gets a free pass in life. Where there is light, there is always dark. It's the genius of *Ted Lasso* that the show is never so syrupy that it slides past what it really means to be human. The sensitivity and care with which it tackles mental health makes it unlike any other TV show. "It takes a leap of faith to engage in therapy, as it's a process often filled with challenging emotions," explains Erin Qualey, a licensed therapist specializing in addiction and trauma, writing in *The Los Angeles Times*. "Ambivalence is normal and even expected. Ted Lasso delivers a raw and honest portrayal of how — with the right therapist — a person can overcome their fears and begin to pursue a more hopeful path."

Qualey is not the only person to notice the care that has been taken with the highly sensitive subject. Sudeikis has said that he and the rest of the Lasso writing team receive messages daily from people thanking them for opening their eyes to what it means to go therapy, and how it has helped them in their lives. "Anything that you can do to help yourself helps those around you," Sudeikis has said. "I think that we were trying to explore that and personify it in a way and kind of trojan horse that there's bigger issues in this fun, silly little comedy show."

Co-writer Brendan Hunt believes we owe it to ourselves. "We all should be taking a good, long, hard look at ourselves, figuring out what we are and how we got the way we are… And make damn well sure that we're doing at least something to make what's going on inside a little bit of a better situation."

Psychotherapy, or talk therapy, is said to have been invented by the neurologist Sigmund Freud at the end of the nineteenth century. He described it somewhat stuffily as 'a clinical method for evaluating and treating pathologies in the psyche through dialogue between a patient and a psychoanalyst'. Many of Freud's theories were controversial, both then and now. (Penis envy, anyone?) Fortunately, therapy has come a long way since then. But Freud can be credited for getting the ball rolling on one of the best tools in the psychotherapist's toolbox today. More than a hundred years later, there is substantial proof that the therapy process can help people achieve long term mental health improvement.

At its heart, therapy is about being able to discuss

our concerns and challenges with a person who holds no bias or judgments. By talking honestly, our difficulties can be addressed and treated. Sometimes that can mean simply exploring past experiences so that we can understand ourselves better. Other times it can mean offloading problems that feel overwhelming and finding ways to look at them differently. Sometimes, therapy is also about helping us get past a big traumatic experience. There are different types of therapy too, and many therapists use a combination of techniques. Without getting too caught up in the technicalities, the point is, if we are struggling with interior battles, seeking out the help of a mental health professional could be the greatest, kindest, and most helpful thing we can do for ourselves.

In the end, it is what helps Ted. An incident between Jamie Tartt and Jamie's abusive father in the locker room following a match is the catalyst that gets Ted there. The incident triggers something deep inside of him, which we, the audience, suspect is the cause of his panic attacks and the reason he's been so hostile to Dr. Sharon, wanting to talk to her, aware that she might help, but never quite bringing himself to share what it is that's locked up inside him. Eventually we see him racing to call her, sharing that his father took his own life when Ted was sixteen years old. "I don't know if that's where some of my issues stem from…" he says.

"It definitely is…" Dr. Sharon says, and so Ted eventually lands on her sofa in a therapy session, breaking down in tears and talking about the suicidal death of his father in one of the most powerful scenes of the entire season, earning the show as many accolades from mental health professionals, as acting awards. "I think if he would have known how good he was, he wouldn't have done what he did," Ted tells Dr. Sharon, profound buried pain coming to light in a way that is so realistic, it's not surprising that the show has been credited for helping hundreds of people understand the benefits of therapy. By talking about it, we see how Ted is relieved of some of the burden he has been carrying, and we see how it helps. Dr. Sharon cannot change the past, but she shows Ted a way forward from an awful personal tragedy.

You only need look the scene up on YouTube and read the comments made there, or read conversations about it on Twitter and Facebook, to see how deeply the scene has touched the lives of others. "For a show such as *Ted Lasso* to depict the initial stages of therapy with such care and nuance is an act of generosity," says Qualey. "Just as Dr. Sharon modeled desirable behavior for Ted, the series successfully modeled a very real experience that can and does hold people back from finding the support they need."

But there is a second strand to the subject of mental health which also appears in the same season. After it has been leaked to the press that Ted suffers from panic attacks, we see him being lambasted in the newspapers. His mental health issue is perceived instantly as a weakness, a reason he shouldn't be in the job. A sports coach having panic attacks? What kind of man is that? The public response is abusive and unkind, perfectly demonstrating the real-life stigma that gets attached to mental health concerns. The headlines that Ted garnered are the very reasons too many people feel it is damaging to admit to mental health problems. It is one of the reasons, perhaps, why Ted had kept his own issues quiet.

When the show's writers were drawing up their plans for the second season, the Tokyo Olympics, which took place in July 2021, had not yet happened. But it turned out the writers of the show were prescient in their profiling of mental health issues in sports. That summer, just as the second season went on air, Simone Biles, the USA Olympic Gold gymnast, pulled out of the women's team gymnastics final, shocking the world when she announced to a packed press room: "I have to focus on my mental health and not jeopardize my health and well-being".

She was only 24 years old and risked her reputation by revealing her mental health problems in a world that stigmatized them. "Physically, I feel good, I'm in shape. Emotionally, that kind of varies on the time and moment... We're going to take it one day at a time," she told reporters bravely.

In every sense, she was doing in real life what *Ted Lasso*'s writers were also trying to achieve on screen – tackle the stigma attached to mental health. Biles didn't have to reveal the reasons for her withdrawal from the final. She could have stayed quiet. She could have invented a fictional excuse. But she chose not to.

Instead, she explained to reporters that as the face of the US Olympic team, with a stellar record of Olympic golds, she felt she was shouldering the hopes of her whole country and some heavy-weight expectations when she entered the Olympic stadium. She explained that it was a pressure that she couldn't cope with. "At the end of the day, we're human too," she said, simply.

She wasn't the first athlete to make that salient point either. Only weeks before, tennis star Naomi Osaka had also withdrawn from the French Open, citing long bouts of depression after winning the United States Open in 2018, and explaining that she too had a hard time coping with the pressure of being at the most competitive end of sports. "I do hope that people can relate and understand it's okay to not be okay, and it's okay to talk about it. There are people who can help," she wrote in *Time* magazine afterwards.

Both women's brave and risky admissions, prioritizing their mental health over societal prejudice, seemed to mostly win applause. "We are proud of you, and we are rooting for you," former first lady Michelle Obama told Biles. The Director General of the World Health Organization, Tedros Adhanom also praised Biles for her honesty, calling on others to look after their mental health. "We need to protect it in whatever way works for each of us," he tweeted.

But not everyone's response was kind. Exactly as the show's former coach and TV commentator George Cartrick had weighed in, calling Ted a 'big girl's blouse' for having panic attacks, so real-life television presenter Piers Morgan weighed in on Biles: "Are 'mental health issues' now the go-to excuse for any poor performance in elite sport? What a joke," he tweeted, adding in a newspaper:

"Sorry Simone Biles but there's nothing heroic or brave about quitting because you're not having 'fun' – you let down your teammates, your fans, and your country." He'd been less than sympathetic about Osaka too, calling her an "arrogant spoiled brat."

As shocking as Morgan's public responses were, they were typical of the prejudice and discrimination that mental health issues seem to attract. In 2019, the American Psychiatric Association conducted a poll, looking into the prevalence of prejudice and stigma around mental health, and found that it remains a major challenge in the workplace. Approximately 50% of workers polled said they were concerned about discussing mental health issues at their jobs. More than one in three were concerned about retaliation or being fired if they sought mental health care. Hardly surprising when there are people like Piers Morgan voicing prejudice with a bull horn.

But thanks to people like Biles, Osaka, and many others speaking out, the cultural acceptance of mental health problems is slowly making headway. That's important for all of us because although Biles and Osaka were talking about the extreme pressures they felt as professional athletes, the mental health issues they were experiencing were no different from the mental health issues that anyone can suffer from. Most of us do not need to be heading up an Olympic gymnast team to feel pressure. A nine-to-five job with a nagging boss can provoke the same feeling. Most of us do not need to have the hopes of an entire country on our shoulders to feel the weight of someone else's expectation. A mother-in-law or parent can do that. The point is, we can all find ourselves hiding our problems away for fear of what others might think.

At the end of the second season, after experiencing the harsh judgment of the press on his mental difficulties, Ted decides to tackle the subject head on, in the way that we always knew our hero would. It's the way that Biles and Osaka did too, taking the subject where it needs to go: out into the open. "I'd like to talk about mental health in athletics," Ted says to a room full of press.

It's up to the rest of us now to keep the momentum going, getting past our own resistance to seeking help when we need it, and refusing to stigmatize others, because as Keeley tells Roy's niece Phoebe: "Problems are like mushrooms. The longer you leave them in the dark, the bigger they get."

Ways to Fight Mental Health Stigma.
From National Alliance on Mental Illness.

1. Encourage equivalence between physical and mental illness.
2. Choose empowerment over shame.
3. Be honest about treatment.
4. Let the media know when they are being stigmatizing.
5. Don't harbor self-stigma.

7

BE A GOOD PARENT
(TO YOURSELF)

"BOY, I LOVE MEETING people's moms. It's like an instruction manual for why they're nuts," Ted says when Rebecca invites him to lunch with her mother, highlighting the theme about parental influence, which runs through every season of the show. Our relationships with our parents can be complicated. They're fundamental to who we are and what we become, and they're rarely ever perfect. Sometimes, some of us get shaped with odd angles and difficult edges that cast negative shadows on us as adults. Sometimes, difficult childhoods or traumatic experiences can impact the ways in which we see the world, leaving us unhappy or anxious or angry, and certainly not as carefree as we ought to be. The show tackles the subject head-on.

When Ted finally describes to Dr. Sharon how he came home from school one day to discover his dad's body, the scene is made more powerful when Rebecca also shares a childhood story, underscoring the profound influence our parents have on our lives. At her father's funeral in the church before the service, she tells her mother she is "sick of keeping secrets," revealing how she too came home one day as a teenager to find a horrifying scene. In a clever interplay of words, switching between Ted and Rebecca, we learn that as a young girl, Rebecca was confronted with the unexpected sight of her father having sex with another woman while her mother was away. Like Ted, she has been carrying the weight of it ever since, keeping it quiet from her mother, bottling it up, where it has festered, making her angry and hating her father. Even now, at his funeral.

Living with the memory of difficult experiences that took place during childhood can be debilitating. It can also shape us, sometimes turning us into bullies, like Jamie Tartt. By the second season, we come to sympathize with Jamie. He has been enduring cruel behavior from his abusive, bullying father for years. In the Wembley locker room after the team loses to Manchester City, his dad taunts him, calls him names and embarrasses him in front of his teammates. We understand why Roy hugs Jamie when he finally punches his dad, because we want to hug him too.

For all his shortcomings, Jamie's most endearing charm is that he is trying to get past a difficult relationship with his father. We learn how difficult that has been in the third season when we meet Jamie's mom. We also see it in Ted when his mom comes to visit. But psychologists believe that getting out from the shadow of a less than ideal parent, or getting past a difficult childhood, is not impossible. We see that in the show. There is growing support to the idea that we can learn to reparent ourselves and in so doing learn to get past our pasts. "Your true self is so much more than your family role," explains clinical psychologist Lindsay Gibson, PsyD., author of the best-seller *Adult Children of Emotionally Immature Parents: How to Heal from Distant, Rejecting or Self-Involved Parents* (New Harbinger Publications). "Your past identity may have been formed in your relationship with your parents, but who you will become derives from your relationship with yourself."

Gibson argues that emotional loneliness in adult life is a tipoff that one's relationships in childhood were not nurturing or supportive enough. "If we have suffered emotional deprivation, we will be familiar with feeling unseen. A lack of social confidence is another cardinal sign of growing up in an emotionally depriving environment… If you often feel emotional lonely, the first thing is to understand is that your feelings have good reason, that it was never about you being deficient or unlovable. It was about you being emotionally deprived."

Children crave active, interested engagement by the adults in their lives. "When a parent takes the time to get into a back-and-forth engagement with their child, the child feels worthy and lovable," Gibson explains. "When parents reach out for their children, and honestly enjoy their company, a powerful message is sent to that child that he or she matters. As children, we all want to feel as essential to our parents as they are to us. Without this reassurance, we are left adrift in emotional loneliness."

In its simplest form, reparenting is learning how to be very kind to ourselves and loving ourselves like the very best, kindest, most attentive parent ever would. It's self-love in its truest sense. Most of us tend to be protective and defensive around our childhood experience, explains clinical psychologist Dr. Nichole LePera, author of *How to Do the Work: Heal from Your Past, and Create Your Self* (Orion Spring), which addresses how adverse childhood experiences and trauma live with us, activating stress responses that can turn into self-sabotaging behaviors. "But the truth is we have an opportunity to heal and consciously choose different behavior as adults, regardless of what we have experienced in our past. This process is called reparenting. It is the act of giving yourself what you didn't receive as a child. Anyone can begin the process of reparenting themselves. It takes time, commitment, and patience… but it will allow you to heal and forgive."

The idea of reparenting was developed initially in the Sixties by therapists and social workers who were using regression techniques to treat schizophrenia. With some measured success, it grew to be a form of psychotherapy in which a therapist assumes the role of a surrogate parental figure, building trust and treating difficulties often caused by dysfunctional parenting. Over time, the idea has been incorporated and developed into many different therapy techniques, and it has also become a useful self-help tool with many books written on the subject. It is worth stating that while reparenting can be a useful goal, some traumas and backgrounds still require additional professional help. It is important not to oversimplify matters here. When Ted eventually seeks help from Dr. Sharon, it's professional help that makes the difference for him.

"We can start reparenting ourselves by identifying what we need. What didn't you learn in childhood?" says psychotherapist Sharon Martin, MSW, LCSW, author of *The Better Boundaries Workbook and Navigating the Codependency Maze* (New Harbinger Publications). "Which of your emotional needs weren't met? Sometimes the answers to these questions are obvious and sometimes we don't know what we don't know." She suggests looking at areas like self-care, recognizing unhealthy relationships, unhealthy habits and how well or badly we cope when things don't go our way. If we see patterns of behavior in ourselves that don't serve us, that's where we can start to try to do things differently.

Reparenting is not about blaming our parents. Chances are our parents will have endured difficult parenting themselves. It's about forgiving them, loving ourselves, and in so doing rediscovering our potential. By the end of the third season, we see Rebecca, Jamie, and Ted find some peace in their parental relationships. Jamie even finds resolution with his dad; and Nate, who has also had a less than perfect relationship with his father gets an apology when his dad confesses that he didn't know how to parent him. As Ted says, with a little love and forgiveness in our hearts, there are always possibilities.

Simplified Reparenting Ideas

1. Take a good look at your accomplishments and give yourself some praise.
2. Do something kind for yourself.
3. Remind yourself that your feelings matter and so do you.
4. Look for behaviors in your life that don't serve you.
5. Don't be hard on yourself. None of us are perfect.
6. Try to find healthy relationships based on trust.
7. See a therapist.
8. Read *The Better Boundaries Workbook and Navigating the Codependence Maze* by Sharon Martin, MSW, LCSW. (New Harbinger Publications)

8

BE MORE LIKE A WOMAN

"WOMAN UP!" TED tells Jamie, once more back on the Richmond team in the second season.

"I think you mean, 'Man up!'" Jamie replies.

Coach Beard and Ted shake their heads. No, Ted meant what he said. "You've been manning up for a while now," he tells him. "And look where that's got you!"

In a show where stereotypes are challenged, we'd expect nothing less from Ted. He is bringing our attention to the subject which has won the show much praise, the one that makes Ted a hero unlike any other, the one that he confronts so valiantly using wit, not muscles.

There are few places where toxic masculinity thrives better than a men's soccer locker room. It is where 'manliness' conforms to society's expectations that you must be tough, powerful, fearless, and anti-feminine if you are any kind of real man at all. It's where the prejudicial trope permeates. Anything less than being a red-blooded, hulking, macho male, and you are perceived as weak. Men's sports teams are notorious for it.

But that trope, which encourages homophobia, misogyny, and aggression as a by-product, hurts men as much as it does women and the rest of society. Studies investigating attitudes concerning masculinity found that men who had stereotypical views were more negative about seeking mental health services, less likely to get preventative health care generally and more likely to take greater risks with their health. (*Journal of Health and Social Behavior, 2011, Social Science and Medicine, 2007, Psychology of Men and Masculinity, 2015*) And although men typically report less depression than women, they are 3.5 times more likely than women to die by suicide, according to the American Psychological Association. What does that say? It says men feel a pressure to stay tight-lipped about mental health issues until they are too much to bear, and the only way out appears to them to be suicide.

The issue is so pervasive that in 2019 the American Psychological Association published their first-ever guidelines to help psychologists work with men and boys. Drawing on more than 40 years of research, they wrote that traditional masculinity – marked out by stoicism, competitiveness, dominance, and aggression – is psychologically harmful, and socializing boys to suppress their emotions causes damage that echoes both inwardly and outwardly. "Because of the way many men have been brought up – to be self-sufficient and able to take care of themselves – any sense that things aren't okay needs to be kept secret," explains Fredric Rabinowitz, Ph.D., psychologist at the University of Redlands, who worked on the guidelines. "Part of what happens is men who keep things to themselves look outward and see that no one else is sharing any of the conflicts that they feel inside. That makes them feel isolated. They think they're alone. They think they're weak. They think they're not okay. They don't realize that other men are also harboring private thoughts and private emotions and private conflicts."

Cultural pressures for boys and men to be tough are everywhere, not just in sports locker rooms. 'Big boys don't cry' is a mantra that boys hear from an early age, teaching them to suppress emotion internally. 'Man up' is another particularly damaging phrase because it is used as an emotional silencing tool. Frequently, to be a man seems to mean living up to hypermasculine expectations, which is why tackling the subject on a TV show offers hope for the future and demonstrates the writers' bravery.

From the very first moments of the first episode when Rebecca fires George Cartrick, AFC Richmond's coach before Ted's arrival, played by Bill Fellows, the battle cry against toxic masculinity goes up. "I love what you've done to the place," George says, walking into Rebecca's office. "Did you do it yourself or get some poof to help you?" George is a man's man who has been hardened by years of male locker room talk, casually homophobic, misogynistic, and so sure of his strident masculinity that he thinks he can patronize his new female boss. "Right love, I've got training in a minute, so whatever it is you need to get off your…" he gestures crudely at her breasts, "impressive chest, let me have it."

So she does, firing him in one of the sharpest and funniest put-downs on TV, while we cheer and root for Rebecca, because most of us have met men like that - men who feel they must degrade a woman in order to be seen as masculine. And with the firing of George comes the opening of the door to a new coach, a man who is not afraid to admit that he cries, was once scared of dogs, who makes cookies, who gives the team books as gifts, who covers up a picture of Keeley's naked breasts in the locker room.

The contrast between Richmond's old coach and the new one tells us everything about the depravity of toxic masculinity. By the second season, George has found himself a new job as a sports commentator. Now we see him on a TV panel discussing his former team: "Richmond is like a woman behind a wheel. Totally lost," he says, as misogynistic and egotistical as ever. But in the same episode we see Ted in the locker room discussing romcoms with the team. It's a striking divergence, and do we think less of Ted as a man as a result? In fact, we love him more for it. Ted would never be as crude as his predecessor, he would never put a woman down, and as reporter Trent Crimm points out: "In a business that celebrates ego, Ted reigns his in." Of the two coaches, we respect Ted more than we ever would George because Ted has found the strength to break the stereotype mold. He has thrown out the male rivalries on his team and made the locker room a healthier, happier place by giving men the space to share their feelings, even to the extent that they can admit that they watch romcoms.

The genius of the show also makes us ask this question: if all men were given space to unbutton their emotions and be less bound up in stereotyped masculinity, what would the world look like? In each of the parent-child relationships that the show highlights – Jamie's, Rebecca's, Nate's and Ted's – it is the father who comes under scrutiny. It is the father's behavior that seems to damage the life of his offspring, as well as hurt his own. Ted's father who committed suicide fits precisely into the statistics - men who can't share their feelings and finally feel so overwhelmed that they can't go on. Ted wishes that his father had talked to him and promises himself that he'll never be a quitter, nor quit on other people. It partly explains why he is who he is and why he becomes the character to tackle toxic masculinity head on.

The term 'toxic masculinity' can be traced back to the eighties when psychologist Shepherd Bliss, Ph.D., began to challenge the ideas of traditional masculinity. "From the Marlboro Man on billboards to Sylvester Stallone on screen and Ronald Reagan in the White House... the man they assert is supposed to be tough, hide his feelings and remain in charge. As a result, many men feel conflicting pressures," Shepherd wrote in 1987, becoming one of the leaders in what was known as the Mythopoetic Men's Movement, which challenged archetypal mythology ideas like warrior kings. Shepherd identified several common male behaviors that he described as toxic to masculinity: extreme self-reliance, that is being unable to ask anyone else for help; shame at expressing emotion, extreme aspiration for physical, sexual, and intellectual domination, devaluation of women's opinions and bodies, and condemnation of anything feminine seen within another man.

By 2017, those traits were still pervasive in society, but further research had found the extent to which they harmed men. A study called The Man Box Report collected far-reaching data from young men, aged between 18 and 30, living in Mexico, United Kingdom, and United States. It found that men's health and well-being were seriously being compromised by these traits. Researchers working on the study used the term Man Box to describe the rigid construct of cultural ideas about male identity, including being self-sufficient, acting tough, sticking to rigid gender roles, being heterosexual, having sexual prowess, and using aggression to resolve conflicts. They found that men who lived inside the Man Box suffered more mental health concerns than men who lived outside it. Those men also practiced riskier behaviors, particularly binge drinking and reckless driving, and they were more prone to violence and bullying. In the US and UK, men who were defined as being in the Man Box were as much as six or seven times more likely to report having perpetrated acts of online or physical bullying against male peers.

"Men who adhere to the rules of the Man Box are more likely to put their health and well-being at risk, to cut themselves off from intimate friendships, to resist seeking help when they need it, to experience depression, and to think frequently about ending their own life," the report stated.

For women, the landscape has shifted in recent decades. Not perfectly, by any means. But with social movements like #MeToo, and greater emphasis on girls being told that they can achieve anything they want if they set their minds to it, female stereotyping is very slowly being reimagined. That's reflected in the show too: Keeley confesses that she used to worry that she might end up like her mother, spending years working at the same company, letting a man take the credit and not being brave enough to dream big. Rebecca too is heralded as a 'Badass Boss'.

In schools and the workplace, studies show that girls now typically outperform boys. So where does that leave men? Possibly still trapped in the same suffocating models of masculinity, feeling threatened and confused. What do all the school shootings that have blighted American society for the last two decades have in common? Angry boys. Almost not a single female shooter.

The issue gets even more complicated when race and sexuality are considered. The 2015 National School Climate Survey found that 85 percent of LGBTQ+ students reported being verbally harassed at school over their gender expression or sexual orientation. African American and Asian-American men are also particularly susceptible to toxic masculinity, according to studies.

So, what is the answer? Given that toxic masculinity appears to be passed down through generations, raising boys without perpetuating the idea that being tough is the only way to be strong seems a good start. Raising kind, gentle caring men who are strong enough to cry and smart enough to understand that it's fine to ask for help can only improve society. We also need to stop shaming men when they express an emotion other than anger.

When Ted has his team watching the movie *The Iron Giant*, the night before their big match with Everton, he knows he is going to have a room full of crying men. Was that deliberate? Of course it was. He knows that encouraging a full soccer team of men to weep openly in front of each other and being in touch with their emotions is only going to serve them well.

How to Avoid the Toxic Masculinity Trap and 'Woman up!'

1. Avoid the phrase 'Man up'. There are many ways to be a man that do not involve sexism, oppression, and aggression. Reimagine what being a man means.

2. Avoid perpetuating the myth that boys don't cry. Instead, acknowledge that crying is fine. Sometimes, it can even be good for you.

3. Acknowledge that feeling vulnerable is not a weakness. It's normal. As Keeley says to Roy: "You being passionate and vulnerable is fucking hot."

4. Do not confuse acting tough with being strong. The two things are not the same.

5. Practice asking for help when you need it. It does not make you less of a man.

6. Learn to wear your heart on your sleeve. Talking about your feelings is better than bottling them up.

7. Be your true self, not society's idea of what that should be.

8. It takes mental strength to care for your mental health. Reach out to professionals if you need to.

9. Stop reproducing outdated masculine attributes like violence and aggression.

10. Educate yourself about what masculinity really means, and be a leader, like Ted.

9

BE FORGIVING

REBECCA IS SORRY. She realizes she has done wrong. She knows she must come clean, but 'sorry' is the hardest word. She invites Ted into her office to tell him how misguided she has been, but she just can't bring herself to say it. She visits him in the locker room, but still, she can't find the words. It's the end of the first season. She must say sorry.

Eventually, it takes her ex's cruelty and recognizing her own feelings of hurt before she comes to her senses. "Ted, I lied to you," she blurts out, her misdemeanors tumbling out like confessions in a church. She tells Ted she hired him because she wanted Richmond to fail, and she's been sabotaging him every chance that she's had. She did it because the club is all that Rupert, her ex, cares about. She wanted to destroy the club to cause Rupert as much pain and suffering as he had caused her. She was so angry, she didn't even care who she hurt in the process.

What an insult to Ted's coaching skills to hire him only because she imagined he'd fail! She scarcely dares look him in the eye. She is frightened now that he will be angry with her. He'd have every right to be. But our hero doesn't hesitate. Not even for second. He forgives her straight away. He even makes it easy for her, giving her the excuse that divorce makes folks do crazy things – like coaching soccer in London, for heaven's sakes. "You and me, we're okay," he tells her.

Of course he forgives her. That's Ted all over. He is someone who allows compassion for someone else to come before his own ego and sense of pride. Perhaps he also knows that feeling aggrieved and offended, allowing an insult to turn into a lingering resentment, will only hurt him.

Remaining angry with someone confines us to a state of victimhood, according to psychologists. The only way to experience healing and peace is to forgive, said the late South African archbishop Desmond Tutu in his book: *The Book of Forgiving* (Harper Collins). "Until we can forgive, we remain locked in our pain and locked out of the possibility of experiencing healing and freedom, locked out of the possibility of being at peace."

It's a message supported by philosophers, psychologists, and psychotherapists everywhere. When we hang onto the hurt and resentment of what another person might have inflicted on us, then we are allowing them to cause further damage in our lives. Remember Ted's message to Sam about being a goldfish, right at the start? Those negative feelings that we hold onto can fester and aggravate. They can continue to damage us for years unless we let them go.

Studies show that people who report higher levels of forgiveness, also have better health habits and decreased anxiety levels. (*Forgiveness, Stress and Health, Annals of Behavioral Medicine. 2016*).

But finding forgiveness isn't easy. In the locker room after Jamie Tartt has rejoined the team, he is humbler because he has nowhere else to go and grateful for Ted's generosity in having him back. But the other players are filled with resentment at his return. They are not ready to forgive. Sam says that no teammate had ever made him feel as bad about himself as Jamie did. "You called me a jaundiced worm in a profile for my hometown newspaper," says Colin Hughes, played by Billy Harris, another of the players. Jamie had been cruel and unkind to each of them. Roy Kent especially hates him because of his divisive bullying. The final insult was Jamie scoring the winning goal for Manchester City when he was on the opposition team playing Richmond. No team member wants Jamie back.

"I know I wasn't the greatest teammate; I did some shitty things, I said some shitty things, but I want you to know I'm truly sorry," he says, meekly. But the team remains hostile. Sometimes, some acts feel too egregious to be forgiven. We might think the other person doesn't deserve forgiveness. We might think that our forgiveness will be interpreted as approval for poor behavior and so encourage it to continue; we might see forgiveness as being weak, or we might just be too plain angry.

Shock and anger often come before forgiveness, explains clinical psychologist Rubin Khoddam Ph.D., who writes about the power of forgiveness in *Psychology Today. (The*

Psychology of Forgiveness. September 2014). It's worth giving yourself space to respect that process, he argues. But then you must think again to free yourself. "The truth is that forgiveness is more powerful than you might think. Just like anything in life, there are costs to your choices. Staying angry, resentful, and vengeful comes at a price. All these feelings can have a detrimental impact on your physical and emotional heath."

He believes that there are many definitions of forgiveness. What makes it easier to do is to understand that forgiveness does not have to mean being best friends with someone who hurt you. It can sometimes simply mean a recognition and acceptance that you can't change the past and moving on from it. Khoddam lists some common components of what finding forgiveness can mean: gaining a more balanced view of an offender and an event, decreasing negative feelings towards an offender, and trying to increase compassion, giving up the right to punish an offender or demand restitution.

Several episodes later, the Richmond team eventually forgive Jamie. It helps when he supports Sam in his stand against Dubai Airlines. It helps even more when they witness the brutality and meanness of Jamie's father in the Wembley locker room. They come to see that Jamie needs compassion, not further punishment.

Forgiveness is a fundamental component of the show's DNA which continues right through to the very end of all three seasons. (See final chapter).

But it's not just in the big story lines. Apologies are scattered through every episode like a trail of bird-crumbs on a secret forgiveness messaging trail, waiting for us in the audience to pick up on. Keeley says she's sorry to Roy after she bids for him at the benefit night auction to make Jamie, who she was dating at the time, feel jealous, but realizes that she had inadvertently made Roy feel used. Roy forgives her. After writing an exposé about Ted getting panic attacks, Trent Crimm seems to have a crisis of conscience and provides Ted with his source. Ted forgives him. Rebecca apologizes to Higgins for treating him badly, and to her god-daughter Nora and best friend Sassy for abandoning them. They forgive her too. Roy's niece, Phoebe, apologies to Roy for swearing at school, and Roy apologizes to her for swearing all the time. Sorry, sorry, sorry. These are small, detailed touches which add to the sweetness of the show, but they also show us a way to be kinder and more considerate in our own interactions with others.

But how do you forgive a perpetrator who has done more than just be thoughtless? How do you forgive someone who might have murdered your family or abused you or violated you? How do you forgive the unforgivable? Real life has a habit of being more challenging than a TV comedy. The late Archbishop Desmond Tutu would argue that's when forgiveness becomes even more important.

He would know. He was the chairman of South Africa's Truth and Reconciliation Commission, created by Nelson Mandela in 1995 to help South Africans come to terms with their extremely troubled past, providing support to the victims of some of the violations and atrocities that took place under apartheid. Through his work, he saw first-hand how forgiveness was essential for healing. "I don't like to talk about my own personal experience of forgiveness, although some of the things people have tried to do to my family are close to what I'd consider unforgivable," he explains in his writings. "I don't talk about these things because I have witnessed so many incredible people who, despite experiencing atrocity and tragedy, have come to a point in their lives where they are able to forgive.

"When I talk of forgiveness, I mean the belief that you can come out the other side a better person; a better person than the one being consumed by anger and hatred. Remaining in that state locks you in a state of victimhood, making you almost dependent on the perpetrator."

Archbishop Tutu became one of the founders of The Forgiveness Project, a UK based charity, which actively collects stories from both victims and perpetrators of crime and conflict everywhere who have rebuilt their lives following hurt and trauma. The charity provides resources and experiences to help anyone examine and overcome their unresolved grievances. The stories of hurt on their website are heartbreaking, but astonishing for the level of forgiveness, giving testament to the human ability to forgive in the most difficult of circumstances, and the healing that can take place as a result.

At the end of the second season, Ted asks his team to forgive him for not coming clean about his panic attacks earlier. "Now, I hope y'all can forgive me for what I've done. 'Cause I sure as heck wouldn't want any of y'all to hold anything back with me." In that moment, we see Ted's need to ask for forgiveness, his understanding how vital it is.

"Nah," says Isaac. "We got you, Coach."

Thoughts on Forgiveness

"As I walked out the door toward the gate that would lead to my freedom, I knew if I didn't leave my bitterness and hatred behind, I'd still be in prison."
—NELSON MANDELA.

"Forgiveness is giving up the hope that the past could have been any different, it's accepting the past for what it was, and using this moment and this time to help yourself move forward."
—OPRAH WINFREY.

"Nothing is easier than to condemn the evildoer, nothing is harder than to understand him."
—FYODOR DOSTOYEVSKY.

"Darkness cannot drive out darkness; only light can do that. Hate cannot drive out hate; only love can do that."
—MARTIN LUTHER KING, JR.

"You never really understand a person until you consider things from his point of view… Until you climb inside of his skin and walk around in it."
—ATTICUS IN TO KILL A MOCKINGBIRD.

"To err is human; to forgive, divine."
—ALEXANDER POPE.

"One of the greatest gifts you can give yourself, to forgive."
—MAYA ANGELOU.

"To be wronged is nothing, unless you continue to remember it."
—CONFUCIUS.

"Be a goldfish."
—TED LASSO.

10

BE YOU

REBECCA IS ON the sofa in her office, looking at her phone. She has been exchanging texts with a mystery man on a dating app called Bantr which Keeley has introduced her to. The mystery man is quoting the Austrian poet Rilke, musing that our deepest fears are like dragons guarding our deepest treasures. Rebecca is moved.

The selling point of the app is that it contains no photos. Users get to know potential dates based on conversation, and what they write to each other, not based on what they might look like. As ever, the show is reinforcing the idea that judging books by their covers is to be avoided, and Austrian poetry adds to the romance of it. Keeley describes the app as "a place where minds come to undress."

But even a blind dating app still requires its users to present themselves in one way or another. Keeley tells

Rebecca that even when it comes to love, it's all about pro-moting your own brand. Rebecca is mystified. Do we really need to brand ourselves like a product to find someone?

She asks Higgins how he branded himself when he first met his wife. He tells Rebecca that he was attempting to be a brooding punk when he first met his wife, Julie, more than 29 years before. When "She's a Rainbow," by the Rolling Stones came on, he started playing upright air bass with a full beer glass in his hand and ended up pouring the beer over his head. Everyone in the pub laughed, except for the one person who handed him a bar towel and he later married. "I suppose the best brand is being yourself," he concludes, making the point that when we try to be anything other than ourselves, we can end up making fools of ourselves.

It's a timely and vital message. We live in a culture of comparison where there are serious pressures, particularly for teenagers and young adults, to present themselves as perfect. If it is not air-brushed images in magazines telling us we need to look a certain impossible way, it is social media telling us how we ought to be living out our perfect, happy lives, gathering 'likes', 'friends' or 'fol-lowers' as we go. If we are not achieving 'likes', it is easy to think we must be 'less than.' If we don't look like an airbrushed size zero model then we can't be attractive; if we're not out partying in the club or vacationing on a tropical island, then our lives must be worthless.

In a high-tech, hyper-digital age filled with unrealistic expectations and pressures to conform on social media, it is easy to doubt ourselves and even harder to simply be ourselves. It explains why rates of depression and anxiety among teenagers and young adults are rising, according to psychologists. It is also why our social media profiles become presentations not of who we are, but of who we think we ought to be. "Revealing our true selves can feel like a huge risk now that we live in a world where everyone is presenting themselves as perfect, attractive and happy online," explains psychologist Tchiki Davis Ph.D., author of *Outsmart Your Smartphone: Conscious Tech Habits for Finding Happiness, Balance, and Connection IRL* (New Harbinger Publications). "We think no one would possibly like us for who we really are."

But being ourselves – being authentic to ourselves – is useful if we want to find contentment. In 2014, Louisiana Tech University conducted a study in which they measured the correlation between life satisfaction and feelings of authenticity, demonstrating that if you can be authentic, as in behaving in accordance with your true thoughts, beliefs, personality, and values, then you're more likely to be happy *(Authenticity, Life Satisfaction, and Distress: A Longitudinal Study. July 2014.)*

"Your time is limited, so don't waste it living someone else's life," advised the late Apple Founder, Steve Jobs at a Stanford University commencement ceremony in 2005. "Don't be trapped by dogma – which is living with the results of other people's thinking. Don't let the noise of others' opinions drown out your own inner voice. And most important, have the courage to follow your heart and intuition. They somehow already know what you truly want to become."

As someone who is regarded as one of the great original thinkers, who took one of the most creative and adventurous journeys himself, his words carry some weight. Rather than fit the mold or conform, he remained true to himself and founded one of the most successful computer companies in history.

Being true to ourselves seems to be another message written into the show. When Isaac McAdoo, played by Kola Bokinni, becomes captain of the team, we see him struggle with his new role, uncertain of himself. He's a "wigwam and a teepee right now," according to Ted when he recruits Roy, now retired, to help him set McAdoo straight. They meet at the soccer field where Roy learned to play soccer when he was growing up. "I brought you here to remind you that football is a game you used to play as a kid because it was fun," Roy grunts at McAdoo. "So f*** your feelings, f*** your overthinking, f*** all that bullshit. Go back out there and have some "f***ing fun." At the next match, we see McAdoo with a smile on his face again. He is playing silly games with the rest of the team during the warm-up, and we get a sense that McAdoo has unleashed his true self. He had got lost, caught up in conforming to the role he imagined a captain should follow, instead of being himself.

But he is not the only character to realize that authenticity is everything. Watching McAdoo come alive again on the soccer field reminds Roy how he too has strayed from who he really is. He's taken a job commentating on matches from a TV studio, which he's not enjoying. When he sees McAdoo playing better on the field because of his advice, he realizes that he needs to get back to where his heart really is. "Sorry fellas, this isn't what I'm meant to do," he tells the other commentators, pulling off his microphone and walking off set. For several episodes of the second season, Ted had been asking Roy to return to Richmond as a coach, and Roy had fought against it. Now he realizes that being in a sterile TV studio does not suit him. For him to be happy and true to himself, he needs to be out in the cold, on the side of a soccer field.

Discovering who we are and not doubting ourselves can sometimes be a trick, but it's not an impossible one. The key is avoiding forced behavior like people-pleasing and being run ragged trying to fulfill other people's expectations. "We spend so much of our time pleasing others that we lose ourselves," says Stephen Joseph Ph.D., writing in *Psychology Today (Are You True to Yourself? Authentic People Know Their Boundaries. October 2018)* "But the truth is that many of us are a lot more powerful than we dare to let ourselves know."

"Listen to your gut, and on the way down, listen to your heart and between those two things, they'll let you know what's what" – Ted.

1. Don't worry about what others think or say about you.
2. Do not compare yourself to others. Compare and despair. You are you.
3. Forgive yourself. We all make mistakes. Learn from them. Don't dwell. Then move on.
4. It is easier to be true to yourself if you know who you are. Try new things, push yourself, be curious and outward looking and you'll find out.
5. Don't aim to please others all the time. People pleasing is exhausting and never earns the respect you hope for.
6. Look for your strengths and focus on positive thoughts about yourself.
7. Be honest.
8. Express your individuality.
9. Stand up for yourself.
10. Get off your phone.

11

BE A GOOD LEADER

BY SEASON THREE, Trent Crimm is no longer working for *The Independent*. He's following Ted around to write a book about AFC Richmond, and after he's been observing him a while, he has a lightbulb moment. "It's going to work," he says excitedly. "You haven't switched tactics in a week, you've done this over three seasons…" Ted smiles knowingly. "…And you've done it by slowly but surely building a clubwide culture of trust and support through thousands of imperceptible moments."

We chuckle to ourselves because while Crimm is referring to three soccer seasons, we have been watching three TV seasons of the show, loving every one of those "imperceptible moments" which have cultivated the culture of trust that Crimm is talking about. But while Crimm imagines that he's talking about a real-life soccer strategy based on trust, called "Total Football" which AFC Richmond has adopted, we know that consistently building trust is what Ted is about at every level. It's what makes him such a good leader.

Whether it is coaching a soccer team, directing a sales force, building a business, teaching at a school, working with volunteers, or just trying to be a good champion of others, empathetic leadership, encouraging a culture of trust and support, has been proven, over and over, to lead to loyal, motivated, creative, happier team members who are more likely to succeed at their goals. (Forgive the pun!) Through three seasons, we see how Ted is a leader the team can trust. It is why the show has earned so much praise from business leaders, who use it as a master class in contemporary leadership.

"At a time when many leaders focus on how they look, want to take credit for collective successes, or see their people as a means to an end, Ted Lasso demonstrates again and again that he is less important than his team and that it's people who matter," explains Marshall Bergmann, leader of the sales team at the Neuro Leadership Institute, advisors to Fortune 500 organizations around the world. "Traditionally, leaders are expected to have all the answers and tell employees what to do. But Ted isn't that kind of leader. He builds a culture of trust and support, and his actions demonstrate how much he values relatedness, teamwork, and helping people achieve their potential. He cares about empowering people to be the best versions of themselves."

Remember the personality clashes and rivalries in the

first season? Ted had landed in a workplace made poisonous by aggression, bullying, and personal resentments at AFC Richmond. But by the third season, the team is united. They root for each other. They share confidences. They trust and like each other so well that when Sam's restaurant is vandalized, the team works to rebuild it; when Colin is fearful that he will experience homophobia with his announcement that he is gay, the team allays his fears and supports him; when Sam is disappointed because he is not invited to play for the Nigerian international team, the team consoles him. It's no small coincidence that the team also now wins soccer matches.

"Ted reminded me of Lou Gerstner, who transformed IBM after arriving in 1993 from RJR Nabisco," explains Bruce Avolio, professor of management at the University of Washington's Foster School of Business. "At the time that Gerstner was installed as CEO... I remember many long-time employees of IBM in my neighborhood saying: 'He has no technology background. I don't think he can even turn on a computer!'" Lou Gerstner, now retired, ensured that IBM's market capitalization rose from $29 billion to $168 billion while he was CEO. Just like Ted who knew nothing about soccer, Gerstner might not have known about computers, but he knew about good leadership and how to turn around the fortunes of a business team. "I see the highest bar for effective leadership being stewardship," explains Avolio, "where a leader enables individuals to achieve their highest states of self-determination, even after the leader is gone. Great leading, like great parenting, nurtures self-determination, the ability to make your own decisions, and act without advice."

We see that in episode nine, when Roy Kent, now a coach, addresses the press in Ted's place. Roy has never been fond of the press (his avoidance of them gets him a dressing down from Rebecca), but he volunteers for the job when Isaac McAdoo stuns the soccer crowd by attacking an abusive fan during a match. In a typical Ted move, Roy tells the press a story about a transgression in his own life when he was young. He doesn't condone McAdoo's actions, but he supports him. "Look, I get that some people think that when they buy a ticket, they think they've got the right to yell whatever abusive shit they want at footballers," he says. "But they're not just footballers, they're also people. And none of us know what is going on in each other's lives. So, for Isaac, even though what he did was wrong, I give him love…. And as for why he did what he did, that's none of my f****** business."

The scene is significant because it demonstrates leadership, The *Ted Lasso* Way. Ted has always led by example and Roy has learned from that, mimicking Ted's willingness to share his own vulnerabilities in a story to get a point across while remaining loyal. We see Roy mimic Ted again when he talks quietly to McAdoo after the incident. McAdoo was expecting Roy to yell at him. We were too. Roy's always been the angry one. But, demonstrating the reach of Ted's influence, Roy shows us now that he too can be understanding, gentle, and perceptive.

Leading by example is always better than yelling. "I don't know what happened there, but I do know that whatever it was, isn't what you're really angry about," he says to McAdoo with great insight. "So, trust me, you've got to go deal with that or you're going to f*** up whatever it is you do care about."

Ted looks for the opportunities in every situation to show a better path, according to Avolio. "Time and time again, he seeks out the developmental or performance opportunity, while also delaying judgment. This occurs when he is interacting with his players, his coaches, the people who own and run the team, and even when he enters a local pub near his apartment. He transmits genuine humility, which a lot of leaders are afraid to do."

Roy is not the only one we see step up. By episode seven, Jamie Tartt is delivering team strategies. Ted has increased Jamie's agency so much that now he's not just a great team player, he's also thinking up tactical ideas for the good of the team in their match against Arsenal, which has a three-goal lead. "Stop going *to* me, start going *through* me," he tells everyone as he moves buttons around the white board, sacrificing his beloved position as striker and moving back to midfield. Given that Jamie once had to be told by Ted, "You're so convinced that you are one in a million that sometimes you forget you are one of eleven," we see how far he's come.

Nate's story too shows us what can be gained when leaders listen to everyone within a team and then give them space. Under the previous coach, no one had thought to ask Nate his opinion on the strengths and weaknesses of the players and how best to use them. As the kitman, he had spent years studying the game from the sidelines, observing the players. He knew who was being underused, who had potential, and which strategies might work. But until Ted came along, no one had noticed Nate's own talents or thought to ask his opinion. Thanks to Ted's encouragement, he becomes a highly effective strategic partner on the coaching team, and we see how by giving everyone the space to reveal their strengths and talents, Ted creates a team which has the potential to really succeed. Of course, there is always the risk that good talent can be poached, which happens with Nate. But if loyalty has been encouraged, which we also see when Nate returns, then the team is more likely to stay together.

Ted's inclusion of everyone, regardless of skin color or sexual orientation, is one of his many strengths. Everyone matters to him equally. "The long game for leadership is about having a humane orientation. Ultimately, our most revered and respected leaders possess this orientation," says Avolio. "These leaders can operate at the global level of a *Nelson Mandela* or at the more intimate level of a caring middle manager, an inspiring elementary school teacher, a confidence-building Boys & Girls Club big brother or sister, or a patient, positive youth soccer (a.k.a. football) coach. These leaders, like Ted Lasso, seek to instill a belief that everyone matters. Everyone can win. Everyone *will* win."

Top Leadership Lessons, *The Ted Lasso Way:*

1. Demonstrate positivity and lead by example.
2. Show empathetic concern for the wellbeing of others.
3. Give others the opportunity to foster relationships and grow.
4. Demonstrate consistency.
5. Encourage self-determination.
6. Build self-confidence in others.
7. Foster inclusion and equity.

12

BE KIND

"I ONLY DID the Boy Scouts for a little bit, but I always loved that notion of: 'Leave the campsite better than you found it,'" Jason Sudeikis has said. In three seasons, he did just that, placing a culture of kindness into the zeitgeist so effectively that he, along with several members of the cast, were invited to the White House by the President as part of Biden's mental health initiative in 2023. "It's nuts, man," Sudeikis said. "I don't think my Midwestern sensibilities would even allow my wildest imagination the opportunity to think the thing would become what it's become. Never, never in a million years."

In the final episode of season three, Roy Kent joins Ted's all-male emotional support group, the Diamond Dogs, and asks the question: Can people change? It's a subject that underlines the intrinsic message of the show. Roy says he has been trying to change himself for the last year because he wants to be someone who is better. "But I'm still the same f****** idiot I've always been," he says, with disappointment. Ted insists Roy must have changed because here he is asking for help, something he's been learning to do.

So, the debate begins on whether it is possible for human beings to change. "I don't think we change per se, as much as we accept who we've always been," says Trent Crimm, now a member of the group. Everyone nods their approval. There are no right or wrong answers. Acceptance of who we are is helpful for all of us. Nate insists that people can change for the better but also for the worse, an acknowledgment of his betrayal to Richmond before returning and asking forgiveness. Coach Beard argues that chasing perfection is a fool's errand. Finally, Higgins concludes: "Human beings are never going to be perfect. The best we can do is keep asking for help and accepting it when we can. If you can keep on doing that, you will always be moving forward towards better."

Inspiring people to be their better selves through kindness was always Ted's mission, so a conversation about how much we can change is a neat conclusion. "Trickle-down economics might stink, but trickle-down support smells like pizza, roses, and I assume Viola Davis," Ted says in the second season. By the end, we see the results, holding up a mirror for us to reflect on our own lives.

By episode ten of the third season, Rebecca gives a speech to a group of football club owners that is so generous, heartfelt, and kind that it's only because we have witnessed her journey of transformation that we even recognize her from the 'hot mess' she was at the start. Invited to create a Super League by the billionaire Edwin Akufo, played by Sam Richardson, Rebecca sees his idea for what it is: a greedy attempt to make money at the expense of poorer fans. "How much more money do you really need?" she asks the men around the table. "Why would you consider taking away from the people something that means so much to them... Just because we own these teams doesn't mean they belong to us." It's an emotional moment, particularly because it's woven into another scene with Nate finding his childhood violin and playing Arvo Pärt's "Spiegel im Spiegel," meaning "mirror in mirror," another message, reminding us to reflect upon ourselves.

Influenced by Ted's kindness and support, Rebecca has found her own self-worth. She is stronger now, mended by embracing her flaws, a message tucked into another scene when she visits a psychic and asked if she is familiar with kintsugi, the Japanese art of mending broken pottery with gold dust. "The idea is that we embrace the flaws and imperfections, and in doing so create something much stronger," says the psychic. The metaphor is lost on Rebecca, but it is there for us to pick up on, reinforced when Nate repairs the torn-up "Believe" sign with gold at the very end.

"Everyone has flaws and makes mistakes," explains psychologist Sharon Martin, MSW, LCSW. "The problem isn't that we're imperfect. The problem is we think other people aren't. When we compare ourselves to others, we feel inadequate... Ironically, it's being imperfect that makes us real and relatable." By accepting her imperfections, learning to forgive and receiving kindness, Rebecca becomes more resilient, generous, and kinder herself. She finds friends and learns to nurture others. Like the very best club matriarch we always knew she could be, she ultimately becomes protective of the team's fans, enough to sell 49% of the club to them.

Zipping between the characters as deftly as swift midfielders, the writers demonstrate the same nuances of change across all the characters. Once irate and uptight, Roy Kent becomes so kindhearted he'll wear a bright tie-dyed T-shirt to please his niece; once secretive and anxious, Colin becomes confident enough to reveal that he's gay; once only "famous for almost being famous," Keeley becomes empowered with her own business. Perhaps the most impressive makeover of all is the evolution of Jamie Tartt, no longer a conceited, self-obsessed bully, but an earnest, respectful team player who, as Dani Rojas points out, "puts aside personal glory on behalf of the team."

"I hope that either all of us or none of us are judged by our weakest moments, but rather the strengths we show when and if we are given a second chance," Ted says in episode eleven, and we see what a great gift that was to Jamie. Now much kinder, Jamie shares confidences with Roy on their night out after an exhibition match in Amsterdam; checks in with Keeley like a good friend after a leaked video threatens her career; and visits his abusive father in a rehab facility. "Jamie always had the potential to be this guy, but he was shrouded in so much pain and confusion about himself," says Phil Dunster, who plays him. But he comes to be "driven by love, rather than by hate," and that's what saves him.

Then there's Nate. Not since Judas snitched on Jesus, and Brutus snuck up on Julius Caesar, has a betrayal been felt so keenly as when Nate tears up Ted Lasso's "Believe" sign, leaks the story of Ted's panic attacks to the press, bullies the team's new kitman, Will, and takes a job as manager for Rupert Mannion's new team, West Ham. His betrayal, after all the kindness that Ted gave him, is the dagger that cuts into our hearts. How is Ted to forgive him? How are we? In season three, we get our answers and learn the importance of giving second chances. Testament to the clever writing of the show, Nate's story needed to be complicated to feel real, because as Ted points out, we all contain "multitudes" (a reference to Walt Whitman's 1855 poem "Song of Myself" about us being too complicated to be one thing or another). But redemption was always likely to be at its heart.

At a West Ham press conference at the start of the third season, Nate describes Ted as a "shitty coach," a reference to Ted's unusual choice of taking the Richmond team into the London sewer system to inspire them to create their own internal system of working together. Nate uses it as an opportunity to show how he has turned to the dark side. We wonder if Ted will bite back, but he simply wishes Nate the best and turns his own press conference into jokes about himself. As ever, our hero leads by example, showing a better path with kindness.

It works. As the season progresses, Nate develops a conscience about what he has done, eventually departing West Ham and writing a sixty-page letter of apology to Ted. But while the rest of Richmond forgives Nate, Coach Beard initially refuses and must be reminded that he too was once given a second chance. Coach Beard's loyalty and friendship to Ted has never been explained before. We understand why Ted moved to England, but Beard's choice to go with him is not made clear until he knocks at Nate's door and shares that he too once took a darker path which led to prison. When he was released and had nowhere to go, Ted gave him a place to stay, and when Beard paid back Ted's kindness by stealing his car, Ted gave him a second chance. "Personality isn't set in stone," says psychologist Susan Krauss Whitbourne, Ph.D. "People can learn from their mistakes—and when you give them a second opportunity, you allow them to demonstrate this."

Ultimately, giving and receiving kindness gives Roy the answer to his question about whether people can change. The act has the power to transform, sometimes in ways that we might not realize. That's the legacy that Ted Lasso leaves after the TV is switched off. Even if there are no more seasons of our favorite show. Even if Ted is a fictional character. Because what would Ted Lasso do if he was with you right now? He'd be checking in with you, listening to you, looking for the good in you, remembering your name, getting distracted with a long story, and giving you one of his little green army men. He'd be forgiving, optimistic, positive, but above all, he'd be kind to you.

REFERENCES

Introduction

Man's Search for Meaning - Victor E. Frankl (Beacon Press).

The Power of Positive Thinking: A Practical Guide to Mastering the Problems of Everyday Living - Norman Vincent Peale (Simon and Schuster).

Learned Optimism: How to Change your Mind and your Life - Martin E.P. Seligman, Ph.D. (Vintage).

The American Psychological Association – *http://www.apa.org*

1. Believe

Self-Efficacy: The Exercise of Control, Albert Bandura (Macmillan).

American Psychological Association.

https://www.apa.org/pi/aids/resources/education/self-efficacy

Nature Neuroscience, January 2016.

Self-Efficacy and Why Believing in Yourself Matters - Kendra Cherry. *www.verywellmind.com*

Albert Bandura: Self-Efficacy and Agentic Positive Psychology - Catherine Moore.

www.positivepsychology.com

Awaken The Giant Within: How to Take Immediate
Control of your Mental, Emotional, Physical and
Financial Destiny! - Anthony Robbins (Simon
and Schuster).

2. Be Successful

Coach Wooden's Pyramid of Success: Building Blocks for
a Better Life - John Wooden, Jay Carty (Revell).

http://www.coachwooden.com/pyramid-of-success

The Greatest: What Sport Teaches Us About Achieving
Success, - Matthew Syed (John Murray).

Neil DeGrasse Tyson's StarTalk Radio – Interview with
Jason Sudeikis.

3. Be Curious

Six Surprising Benefits of Curiosity - Emily Campbell.

*https://greatergood.berkeley.edu/article/item/
six_surprising_benefits_of_curiosity*

Empathy Is the Most Important Leadership Skill
According to Research - Tracy Brower (Forbes).

Stanford Encyclopaedia of Philosophy - *https://plato.
stanford.edu/entries/empathy/*

How To Become a More Empathetic Leader - Tim
Stobierski.

*https://www.northeastern.edu/graduate/blog/
become-an-empathetic-leader/*

Sensitive Is the New Strength: Leaders are Taking on a
New Role – Being Human -

*https://www.glassdoor.com/employers/blog/
sensitive-new-strength-in-leaders/*

4. Be Optimistic

Learned Optimism: How to Change Your Mind and Your Life - Martin E.P. Seligman, Ph.D. (Vintage).

The Optimistic Child – A Proven Program to Safeguard Children Against Depression and Build Lifelong Resilience - Martin E.P. Seligman, Ph.D. with Karen Reivich Ph.D., Lisa Jaycox Ph.D., and Jane Gillham Ph.D. (Houghton Mifflin).

Man's Search for Meaning - Victor E. Frankl (Beacon Press).

Interview with Jason Sudeikis - GQ magazine July 2021

5. Be a Do-Gooder

Volunteering and its Surprising Benefits.

https://www.helpguide.org/articles/healthy-living/ volunteering-and-its-surprising-benefits.htm

Study of Volunteerism and Hypertension Risk in Older Adults - Rodlescia S. Sneed and Sheldon Cohen

https://www.ncbi.nlm.nih.gov/pmc/articles/PMC3804225/

Prosocial Spending and Happiness: Using Money to Benefit Others Pays Off.

https://dash.harvard.edu/handle/1/11189976

Happy Money: The Science of Happier Spending - Elizabeth Dunn and Michael Norton. (Simon and Schuster).

The Science of Good Deeds.

https://www.webmd.com/balance/features/science-good-deeds

Volunteering and Health Benefits in General Adults: Cumulative Effects and Forms - Jerf Yeung, Zhuoni Zhang, Tae Yeun Kim.

https://www.ncbi.nlm.nih.gov/pmc/articles/PMC5504679/

Five Reasons Why You Should Volunteer - Dawn Carr, MGS, Ph.D., Psychology Today.

https://www.psychologytoday.com/us/blog/the-third-age/201403/5-reasons-why-you-should-volunteer

Letters to Santa. *https://letterstosantacharity.com*

Thundergong. *https://thundergong.org*

Ted Lasso for Red Nose Day.

https://www.comicrelief.com

Jason Sudeikis is Having One Hell of a Year - Zach Baron, GQ Magazine.

https://www.gq.com/story/jason-sudeikis-august-cover-profile

6. Be Open To Therapy

What Ted Lasso Gets Right About Resistance to Therapy, According to a Therapist - Erin Qualey. The Los Angeles Times.

https://www.latimes.com/entertainment-arts/tv/story/2021-09-10/ted-lasso-season-2-dr-sharon-therapy-jason-sudeikis-sarah-niles

'We're Human, Too' - Simone Biles Highlights Importance of Mental Health in Olympics Withdrawal.

https://www.nbcnews.com/news/olympics/we-re-human-too-simone-biles-highlights-importance-mental-health-n1275224

Naomi Osaka. It's OK to not be OK. Time Magazine.

https://time.com/6077128/naomi-osaka-essay-tokyo-olympics/

Piers Morgan on Simone Biles - The Daily Mail.

https://www.dailymail.co.uk/news/article-9835069/PIERS-MORGAN-Sorry-Simone-boast-GOAT-selfishly-quit.html

Mental Health Stigma Persists in the Workplace, Poll Shows.

https://psychnews.psychiatryonline.org/doi/10.1176/ appi.pn.2019.6b21

National Alliance on Mental Illness.

www.nami.org

7. Be a Good Parent (To Yourself).

Adult Children of Emotionally Immature Parents: How to Heal from Distant, Rejecting or Self-Involved Parents, - Lindsay C. Gibson, PsyD. (New Harbinger Publications).

http://www.drlindsaygibson.com/articles

How To Do the Work: Recognize Your Patterns, Heal from Your Past, and Create your Self - Dr. Nicole LePera (Orion Spring).

https://theholisticpsychologist.com

The Better Boundaries Workbook: A CBT-Based Program to Help You Set Limits, Express Your Needs, and Create Healthy Relationships - Sharon Martin MSW LCSW. (New Harbinger Publications).

https://www.livewellwithsharonmartin.com

8. Be More Like a Woman!

Men and Depression - Fredric E. Rabinowitz, Ph.D.

American Psychological Association, Guidelines for practice with men and boys.

www.apa.org

Revisioning Masculinity - Shepherd Bliss.

https://www.context.org/iclib/ic16/bliss/

2017 Man Box Report - Promondo and Unilever.

https://promundoglobal.org/wp-content/uploads/2017/03/TheManBox-Full-EN-Final-29.03.2017-POSTPRINT.v3-web.pdf

Journal of Health and Social Behavior, Vol 52 - Kristen Springer Ph.D (2011)

Social Science and Medicine, Vol 64 - James Mahalik, Ph.D. (2007)

Psychology of Men and Masculinity, Vol 16 - Omar Yousaf Ph.D. (2015)

9. Be Forgiving

2017 Forgiveness, Stress and Health – a 5 Week Dynamic Parallel Process Study.

https://academic.oup.com/abm/ article/50/5/727/4562559

Psychology Today

https://www.psychologytoday.com/us/blog/the-addiction-connection/201409/the-psychology-forgiveness

www.theforgivenessproject.com

The Forgiveness toolbox - Dr. Masi Noor.

http://theforgivenesstoolbox.com

The Book of Forgiving: The Fourfold Path for Healing Ourselves and Our World - Desmond Tutu and Mpho Tutu (Harper Collins).

10. Be You

Outsmart Your Smartphone: Conscious Tech Habits for Finding Happiness, Balance and Connection IRL - Tchiki Davis Ph.D., Foreword by Melanie Greenberg Ph.D. (New Harbinger Publications)

Authenticity, life satisfaction, and distress: a longitudinal analysis - Güler Boyraz, J. Brandon Waits, Victoria A. Felix.

https://pubmed.ncbi.nlm.nih.gov/25019552/

https://www.rochester.edu/newscenter/ getting-fewer-likes-on-social-media-can-make-teens-anxious-and-depressed-453482/

https://www.psychologytoday.com/us/ blog/click-here-happiness/201810/ how-be-yourself-in-five-simple-steps

https://www.verywellmind.com/i-hate-myself-ways-to-combat-self-hatred-5094676#citation-5

11. Be A Good Leader

Leadership Lessons from Ted Lasso, by Marshall Bergmann. *https://neuroleadership.com/ your-brain-at-work/leadership-lessons-from-ted-lasso*

Lasso on Leadership, Foster Business Magazine, by Ed Kromer, with Bruce Avolio.

https://magazine.foster.uw.edu/features/lasso-on-leadership/#:~:text=The%20show%20and%20the%20character,empowering%20of%20everyone%20around%20him.

12. Be Kind

The Guardiam. 'I'm Please As Pie': Jason Sudeikis on Ted Lasso and Lessons in Kindness *https://www.theguardian.com/tv-and-radio/2023/may/14/jason-sudeikis-interview-ted-lasso*

Sharon Martin, LCSW. Embrace Your Imperfections. *https://sharonmartincounseling.com*

Psychology Today: 4 Reason to Give Someone a Second Chance, by Susan Krauss Whitbourne, PhD.

https://www.psychologytoday.com/us/blog/fulfillment-any-age/201608/4-reasons-give-someone-second-chance#:~:text=Additional%20research%20on%20why%20you,practical%20and%20saves%20emotional%20energy.

If you enjoyed this book, please consider leaving a review on Amazon. Authors survive on their reviews. We appreciate you!

Coming Soon.

THE WOMEN OF TED LASSO

What would you rather be: a panda or a lion? *"Pandas are fat and lazy and have piss-stained fur. Lions are powerful, majestic and rule the jungle,"* Rebecca tells Keeley. Exuding an intimidating power, Rebecca is every inch a lioness. She's also a *'Boss Ass Bitch'* who mentors and becomes best friends with awe-struck Keeley. Their friendship has become a beacon in TV history showing us what can be achieved when women support each other. They tackle serious subjects like female equality and empowerment, but in a way that feels relatable and funny. Find out how to harness Rebecca and Keeley's lioness power for yourself in this fun guide to the women of *Ted Lasso*.

Printed in Great Britain
by Amazon